food for thought food for thought food for thought
food for thought food for thought food for thought
food for thought food for thought food for thought
food for thought food for thought food for thought
food for thought food for thought food for thought
food for thought food for thought food for thought
food for thought food for thought food for thought
food for thought food for thought food for thought
food for thought food for thought food for thought
food for thought food for thought food for thought
food for thought food for thought food for thought
food for thought food for thought food for thought
food for thought food for thought food for thought
food for thought food for thought food for thought

alan murchison alan murchison alan murchison

food for thought food for thought food for thought
food for thought food for thought food for thought
food for thought food for thought food for thought
food for thought food for thought food for thought
food for thought food for thought food for thought
food for thought food for thought food for thought
food for thought food for thought food for thought
food for thought food for thought food for thought
food for thought food for thought food for thought
food for thought food for thought food for thought
food for thought food for thought food for thought
food for thought food for thought food for thought
food for thought food for thought food for thought
food for thought food for thought food for thought

For Fiona, Megan, Kyle, Freya and Mia, thank you for your love, patience and understanding whilst I have been away playing chef

food for thought

cookbook

Chef Experience

all the best

food for thought

ALAN MURCHISON

'We do not stop playing
because we grow old, we grow
old because we stop playing.'

Benjamin Franklin

Foreword by Raymond Blanc
Photography by Mark Law

Credits

Author	Alan Murchison
Photography	Mark Law
Design and Layout	Lisa Foreman
Printing and Binding	Arkle Print

ISBN 978-0-9557883-0-7

First published in 2007 by Alan Murchison Restaurants Ltd

FSC
Mixed Sources
Product group from well-managed forests, controlled sources and recycled wood or fiber
Cert no. SGS-COC-2679
www.fsc.org
© 1996 Forest Stewardship Council

Printed by Arkle Print Ltd.
Printed using vegetable-based inks.
This product is printed on FSC material under chain of custody conditions by an FSC certified printer

'Food, the one common thing in everyone's life that truly awakens the senses, looking at it, smelling it, touching it, oh and the taste, yes the taste, making the journey worthwhile.' Chef Simon Haigh

foreword

Alan first came to work for me as Sous Chef having previously worked under a number of my protégés.

During his four years with me at Le Manoir aux Quat'Saisons I watched him develop tremendously both in and out of the kitchen to become a great master of his craft.

I have been fortunate over the years to have some very talented chefs grace my kitchen and Alan is up there with the best of them. His true passion for food, creativity and attention to detail are second to none.

Alan has a first-class team that work very well together. The ability to motivate and get the very best out of your team is an essential part of running a restaurant and in that area he excels.

In producing his first book Alan has worked extremely hard and the results are stunning. I am very proud to give you a little 'Food for Thought'.

Bon Appetit
October 2007

Raymond Blanc

WHY ? – My own pursuit of excellence

16 to 18 hour days … 6am starts … Pushing all day long … Stressed … under pressure … 50 covers booked for lunch … 60 for dinner. Bloody meat turns up three hours late – motorway jams … storms off the west coast of Scotland … shit, no scallops for lunch … Sweating, from the minute you walk through the door to the minute you leave … Missing your wife and kids … Forgetting birthdays … Losing touch with friends … Black bags under your eyes … Burns … Blisters … Fat Boy Slim on the radio … Red Bull … Coffee … just the hit to keep you going … on and on … Sore feet and the legendary 'chafing' that is 'Chef's Arse'! The Glamorous life as a top chef!

Why do we do it?? If you have to ask that question then you don t understand the mentality of a chef in a fine-dining restaurant. There is not a chef in my kitchen who could not leave tomorrow, work fewer hours for more money and ultimately gain a better quality of life. However, the satisfaction and obsession with gaining new skills while learning this incredible craft begins to define you as a person and becomes such an essential part of who you are, forever! You just can't put a price on that.

It is essential to develop a solid foundation upon which to build our knowledge. The old adage 'a little knowledge is a dangerous thing' could not be more relevant than in the kitchen. Before you can be released into the creative forum, you need to acquire the understanding behind the processes.

Ask me to identify the key attributes required for the success of a chef in my kitchen and the answer, unquestionably, is – Attitude and Passion!

introduction

I have been incredibly fortunate to work with a number of extremely talented and gifted chefs over the years, who have all, in one way or another, shaped the way that I work and the attitude I hope to instil in my guys. The same attributes that I look for in potential chefs are traits that I have found to be beneficial in kitchens I have worked in.

Produce being of the highest quality is the foundation of many kitchens, but none more so than mine. Here at L'Ortolan, we all have a deep-rooted passion for the food and produce we use in the kitchen. It is commonplace for us all to gather around, staring in awe at a 3kg 'rod and line' caught sea bass, firm to the touch, bright eyes, ruby-red gills and not a scale out of place. We caress it as we would a lover and all get that 'buzz' from knowing that this is simply – as good as it gets.

We could buy the fish in already prepped for us, meat ready to go straight into the pan and bread commercially baked and reheated. However, for me, this would hugely compromise everything I believe in and therefore I would undoubtedly lose the creativity and genuine 'craft' of what being a chef means to me.

Imagine: a restaurant full of guests, some of whom will have travelled far to dine with us, on occasion waited for availability and who are full of expectation. It is our mission that guests will leave us not only having had all their expectations met and hopefully surpassed, but with a passion and enthusiasm ignited that will generate a desire to return – then, and only then, have we succeeded in our job.

In pursuit of this success, we introduced the 'Chef's Table', where guests have the opportunity to indulge in around 14 courses with carefully selected wines while experiencing the kitchen 'theatre' during a busy dinner service. The Chef's Table is available to four guests on Friday and Saturday evenings and has been phenomenally successful, encouraging more people to 'share the passion'.

In my view, all chefs should have the understanding and experience of how to break down a whole animal whether that may be a suckling pig, new season lamb or French-farmed rabbit. Understanding how to butcher a whole animal into its composite parts is a critical element of being a chef. The saddle and best end of any animal have always been considered the premier cuts of meat – the easiest to deal with perhaps, but not necessarily with the best flavour and texture.

A real test of any chef would be to take, say, an oxtail, bone it out, stuff and roll it, then caramelise and braise it slowly until it melts in the mouth, the challenge being to confit, braise, tunnel-bone and caramelise – all skills required to produce from the so-called lesser cuts of meat something that can be magical. Possessing the ability to prepare a secondary cut of meat and the talent to cook it in a way that creates the 'wow' factor is such an art.

Being a chef is not about throwing a fillet steak in a pan, adding foie gras and Madeira sauce: where is the challenge in that? It doesn't and in my opinion never would represent a fine chef.

A true chef should be an artist, a craftsman, butcher, baker and fishmonger all in one, not a guy in a white jacket who takes food from packets, applies heat and puts it on a plate. That is not mine or any of my guys' reason for getting out of bed in the morning.

influences & training

I am often asked where I trained to be a chef, and the reply is always the same: I am still training. We as chefs are in the enviable position of continually learning new skills, new presentation concepts, new ingredients, enthusing about ideas thrown in by guys in the team and re-inventing classic combinations that work so beautifully together. Every day is a school day.

My first jobs were in small family-run country house hotels in Scotland, working with some wonderful people such as Adrian Pieraccinni, who gave me my first ever job. He often gave me a stern talking-to when I stepped out of line and also helped develop my love of sports cars.

Selbie and Flora Florence had a huge influence in guiding me through those early days. They could never stand still and were constantly re-investing in their business and the people around them. They are incredible hoteliers with an enormous natural warmth and welcome for their guests. Selbie and Flora have a great understanding of good local food and produce; they and their family are some of the most decent and genuine people you could ever hope to meet.

I got to thinking that at 18 years old I knew a thing or two about food and standards but, oh boy, was I in for a big wake-up call! Inverlochy Castle with 1* Michelin and Graham Newbould at the helm. Graham was a strict old-school chef who was not afraid to tell you how it is, in a way that only a great Yorkshireman can. He had trained classically at the Connaught

and compromise was not in his vocabulary. Graham taught me about exacting standards and quality. The food we were producing at Inverlochy in the late 1980s was amazing. I look back now at the food photos and it still blows me away – precise, clean, meticulous food.

After a couple of years in the wilderness I returned to Inverlochy Castle to work under another head chef, Simon Haigh. Simon stuck his neck out and took a chance on me as I had gone off the rails. For that opportunity, I thank him sincerely.

Simon had a very different background to other chefs I had worked for. Before the castle he had been Raymond Blanc's Sous Chef at the legendary 2* Michelin, Le Manoir aux Quat'Saisons. He had worked in Michelin-starred establishments throughout his career and has a much lighter, more modern approach to food. He also possesses the most controlled manner I have ever encountered in the kitchen.

Simon's style of man-management means he gets the very best out of every chef fortunate enough to work for him – this undoubtedly gets results. If you ever turned up unshaven, a blunt razor would appear from his office and you would be sent off to the staff toilets for a shave, Simon having removed the soap first! Simon is a good friend and a great work colleague. His self-discipline and consistency were the key skills passed to me, and also the kick up the arse I needed to head south.

And so, I moved on – John Burton Race, when at L'Ortolan, had a fearsome reputation. 2* Michelin and big attitude were all I knew of him, but Simon assured me that he had eaten one of the best meals ever at his restaurant and that Mr Burton Race was cooking some of the most exciting food in Britain.

A brilliant meal, an interview and a trial later, I had signed up to work for JBR. John spent most services in his kitchen. He loves a practical joke, possesses a dry, deranged sense of humour and has a low boredom threshold. He changed things constantly – menus, dishes, sections – and used to get quite a buzz out of putting you in the shit.

Some of the restaurant services we had back then would give me nightmares if I experienced them now running my own business. This makes for a very exciting and interesting time for all the right reasons. His flair for Asian cuisine influenced me and is a slant that touches my food to this day.

John is a very creative and naturally gifted chef, not afraid to let you put forward your own ideas for the menu, and sometimes ideas would end up literally being thrown at the wall – but, hey, that was all part of the learning process.

So then Le Manoir came calling. I knew so much about Raymond Blanc and had all the books! I had worked with Blanc-trained chefs for a number of years but nothing prepared me for the standards and attention to detail that are the hallmark of Le Manoir aux Quat'Saisons.

'RB', as Monsieur Blanc likes to be called, is a true genius in every sense of the word. He has created an industry standard, cultivating a work ethic and discipline that are without parallel. The results speak for themselves. I believe that, to date, Le Manoir has produced over 30 chefs who have gone on to achieve at least 1* Michelin in their own right since leaving. He is his own most fierce critic and is always driving himself to take the dream forward to the next level.

I spent over four years at Le Manoir, progressing from Junior to Senior Sous Chef, then latterly becoming Director of the Ecole de Cuisine. I still use Le Manoir as a measure of how far I have come since those early days in Scotland but more importantly also how far I still have to go. RB has been a great support to me since I left Le Manoir and is always available at the other end of the line if I ever need advice.

 A true gentleman and visionary!

Having run my own business now for a number of years, I can look back and see how seriously the people I worked with and alongside have helped shape me as a chef and as a human being.

I am now on the other end, trying to influence and inspire a group of chefs positively. I am very lucky to have some really great chefs in my own kitchen including my current crop:

Will Holland, Robin Gosse, Iain Swainson, Elliot Lidstone, 'Tiger' Barton, Russell Ploughman, Phil Fanning, Simon Jenkins, all form the basis of my senior Kitchen team. Watch this space ..

Alan Murchison

how to use this book & its philosophy

First of all, the purpose of this book is to inspire you and give you ideas. Some of the dishes are very complex and time-consuming – they would challenge even the most talented of chefs – and others are simpler and can be easily prepared without an army in the kitchen.

This book is not aimed at the beginner in the kitchen; a level of competence and understanding has been assumed. It is also worth bearing in mind that all recipes and dishes have been developed and produced in a very well-equipped professional kitchen.

Please use all the recipes and descriptions as a guide only. For example, whether you use turbot or brill in a recipe, the difference in the end result will be negligible; freshness, seasonality and provenance are much more important than following the recipe to the word.

Remember that cooking times can vary greatly depending on ovens, stoves, pans and equipment. When asked how you can tell when something is cooked or ready, my simple answer is by working 16 hours a day for 10 years in a Michelin-starred kitchen! This is not the answer you want to hear. The reality is that you can only learn by trial and error.

Cooking is like making love: there is no substitute for experience. Timing, touch, taste and smell are the key.

Season to your own personal taste. You are going to be eating the food, not me, so please your own palate. Remember you can always add more seasoning, but it is very difficult to take it away.

Last but by no means least, please enjoy the book – even if you just look at the pretty 'cheffy' food pictures.

Mark Law
Photographer

When Alan and Mark first met over 10 years ago, Alan had just taken over from John Burton Race to run his first restaurant, L'Ortolan in Berkshire. Chef and photographer had an immediate rapport, share the same sense of humour and have been friends ever since.

The idea for a book was to showcase the talents of both individuals: Alan's artistry as chef combined with stunning imagery by Mark. Two years and countless hours of hard work later – not just by Alan and Mark but by all the team at L'Ortolan – the result is their first book together, *Food for Thought*.

For almost 20 years, Mark has been producing images for satisfied clients. He works very closely with his clientele, creating advertising, editorial and corporate images that are both effective and attractive, pleasing the customer and fulfilling the brief. Mark specialises in the photography of food and jewellery and is currently working on a number of other projects with some of the United Kingdom's most talented Michelin-starred chefs.

'The success of my business has been the working relationship between my clients and myself. Repeat business is key and the majority of my client base have been with me for over 10 years. Recently my work has appeared in magazines such as *Vogue, GQ, Tatler, Marie Claire* and *OK* as well as several in-flight magazines.

'I hope you enjoy this book as much as Alan and I enjoyed working on it together.'

Julia Charles (Dip.AIT)(Dip.NNP)
Nutritionist

Julia studied Nutrition at the UK School of Naturopathic Nutrition in Surrey, furthering her qualification with a Diploma in Food Intolerance Testing. She practises at The House of Good Health, Henley-on-Thames, Oxfordshire. Believing strongly in empowerment, Julia encourages patients, through a journey of education, to take responsibility for their health and develop the confidence to manage their own healing process.

Julia is a true believer that supporting the body nutritionally does not imply a compromise on the taste and enjoyment of food. Healthy food need not be boring, dull or time-consuming – it should be fun and exciting, a celebration, making healthy food an important part of everyone's life. This book not only identifies a unique flair for bringing together the most delectable marriages of flavour but also illustrates a great respect for the nutritional balance each dish provides.

With a young family, her focus is on cooking fresh, varied, organic and locally sourced produce wherever possible. Julia believes that involving children in the preparation and cooking processes will inspire future generations to enjoy eating healthily.

Julia was delighted when Alan suggested a nutritional involvement in his book. A huge supporter of his approach to food, she feels that the exceptional selection criteria he uses when sourcing raw ingredients for his restaurants are inspirational.

'Savages'

starters

Asparagus

Green & white asparagus charlotte, artichoke mousse, crispy risotto, truffle & Chardonnay dressing

English asparagus is one of nature's most well-balanced vegetables. High in folic acid, potassium, vitamins C and B$_6$, iron and fibre, asparagus is thought to relieve indigestion and has powerful diuretic properties.

Serves 4

Crispy Risotto

(see basics 229)

flour, whisked egg and

breadcrumbs

Charlotte Artichoke Mousse

(see basics 232)

16 white asparagus spears

16 green asparagus spears

Garnish

4 jumbo asparagus spears

truffle dressing

(see basics 210)

pea shoots

12 slices Perigord truffle

Al's advice
It's well worth the wait for the
English asparagus season.

Preparation

The first job is the crispy risotto base. You can make the risotto the previous day and keep it in the refrigerator. When it's cold, cut it into squares, pané and set aside. Don't pané too far in advance or the breadcrumbs will go soggy.

Prepare the artichoke mousse following the basic recipe. Keep the mousse at room temperature until you are ready to set the charlottes.

Blanch the green and white asparagus spears in boiling salted water for 4–5 minutes and refresh.

To assemble the charlottes, cut the asparagus spears into even lengths – they should slightly overlap the tian rings. Make sure that they are packed tightly into the rings, then spoon in the artichoke mousse and place in the refrigerator to set (allow 2–3 hours).

To finish the dish, thinly slice the jumbo asparagus and blanch for 60 seconds. Deep fry the risotto squares at 180°C for 2–3 minutes until golden brown, then season.

Remove the charlotte from the refrigerator 5 minutes before you wish to serve the dish. Dress the plate liberally with truffle dressing.

Avocado

Avocado & asparagus salad, cured Spanish ham, lemon oil dressing

The cured ham that we use in this dish is a little bit special – the top grade of ham produced in Spain, jamón Iberico de bellota. This is not to be confused with the mass-produced serrano hams. The pigs used in bellota ham feed almost exclusively on acorns and grass in the wild. Drying and maturation of the ham then takes a minimum of 36 months.

Serves 4

Avocado Purée

(see basics 37)

Guacamole

(see basics 189)

8 long croutons cut

from a baguette

olive oil

100g bellota ham

8 blanched asparagus

spears

Garnish

50g Parmesan shavings

pea shoots

12 leaves red chicory

pissant leaf

lemon oil dressing

(see basics 38)

Preparation

The first job is to make the avocado purée and guacamole. Do this 2–3 hours before you want to use them to allow the flavours to infuse, and keep them in the refrigerator. To stop the avocados discolouring while you are working, place them in a bowl and cover with milk.

Brush the croutons with a little olive oil and bake them in the oven until golden brown.

Cut the bellota ham into batons, trying not to eat it all as you cut it!

Assemble the dish at the last minute. Dress with lemon oil dressing at the table.

Al's advice

Pata negra is the term commonly used to describe the ham jamón de bellota. It means black foot.

Beetroot & Sea Trout

Beetroot terrine, hot smoked sea trout, beetroot purée & horseradish cream

Sea trout is a well-known 'oily' fish and an excellent source of omega-3. Oily fish also provides us with natural vitamin D which is required for bone density.

Serves 4

Beetroot Terrine

(makes 1 terrine)

4 leaves gelatine

500ml beetroot liquor

48 large slices cooked

beetroot

(see basics 39)

Smoked Sea Trout

4 x 100g paves sea trout

(see basics 13)

Garnish

beetroot purée

(see basics 40)

horseradish cream

(see basics 29)

herb crème fraîche

(see basics 42)

tarragon Dijon mustard

salad cress

trout caviar

Preparation

Make the terrine and smoke the sea trout a day in advance. All the garnishes should be made on the day you want to serve them.

Soften the gelatine leaves in cold water, drain well and set aside. Bring 100ml of the beetroot liquor to the boil and whisk in the gelatine. Stir into the remaining liquor and season to taste. Set aside, but do not allow the jelly to set.

To build the terrine, first line a mould with cling film. Starting with a thin, even layer of jelly, add alternate layers of sliced beetroot and jelly, allowing each layer to set in the refrigerator before applying the next. This is a time-consuming job but the finished result is well worth it. When you have reached the top of the terrine, place it in the refrigerator for 24 hours.

Slice the terrine carefully using a very sharp non-serrated knife. Do this in advance.

Before serving, bring the sea trout to room temperature.

Al's advice
Mackerel and salmon both work
very well as alternative fish.

Bouillabaisse Terrine

Pressed fillets of red mullet, John Dory, sea bass, lobster, confit tomatoes & saffron shallots

This is a really 'cheffy' terrine to make and involves days of planning and preparation. Use the terrine within 24 hours of making to ensure the freshness of the flavours.

Serves 4

Terrine

(makes 1 terrine)

400g red mullet fillet

400g John Dory fillet

400g sea bass fillet

350g native lobster tail

lemon juice

6 pieces baby fennel

2 large confit red peppers

(see basics 44)

24 pieces confit tomato

(see basics 45)

6 large aubergines

olive oil

xeres vinegar

Bouillabaisse Marinade

(see basics 43)

Bouillabaisse Jelly

(see basics 168)

Garnish

28 slices pickled shallots

(see basics 36)

28 black olive cheeks

28 confit cherry tomatoes

(see basics 45)

picked herbs

saffron dressing

(see basics 203)

Preparation

Scale, fillet and pin-bone all the fish. Blanch the lobster tail for 1 minute; refresh and peel. Place all the fish fillets and the lobster tail in the marinade and leave in the refrigerator for 12 hours to infuse.

Make the jelly following the basic recipe. Set aside but do not allow to set.

Blanch and refresh the baby fennel. Prepare the confit red peppers and tomato as in the basic recipes.

Cut the aubergines into four pieces lengthways. Trim as much of the flesh away as possible, leaving an even strip of skin. Sauté in olive oil and deglaze the pan with xeres vinegar.

Grill the fish and lobster under a medium heat, basting with the marinade. Season with lemon juice and set aside.

To make the terrine, line a triangular mould with cling film. Line the terrine with even strips of aubergine, allowing an overlap of skin reaching halfway down the sides of terrine. To build the terrine, layer up the fish, fennel, tomato and pepper to create an even mosaic effect, covering each layer with the melted jelly as you go. Continue until you reach the top of the terrine, then fold over the aubergine skin and place the terrine in the refrigerator. It is very important that you do not press the terrine, or the jelly, which acts as a 'glue', will be squeezed out.

Place in the refrigerator for 12 hours. Slice with a serrated knife and allow to stand at room temperature for 10 minutes before serving.

Crab

Crab & fennel salad, mango salsa, lemongrass jelly & wasabi yoghurt

Use only the largest of cock crabs. The texture and flavour of the claw meat is just amazing. All chefs tend to have their own favourite areas when sourcing crab – Kevin Bartlett, my crab supplier, sources crab only from the Dart Estuary.

Serves 4

Crab Mixture
250g picked white
crab meat
(1 x 2–3kg live cock crab,
if available)
crème fraîche
lemon juice
chopped fresh coriander

Fennel Salad
12 pieces finely
sliced fennel
juice of 1 lime
wasabi to taste

Lemongrass & Galangal Jelly
(see basics 8)

Garnish
4 halves of soft-shell crab
tempura batter
(see basics 22)
mango purée
wasabi yoghurt
(see basics 46)
24 large pieces
diced mango
sliced spring onions
diced red chilli
coriander cress

Preparation

This is actually a very simple dish to prepare and finish. I cannot over-emphasise the importance of the quality and freshness of the crab.

To cook the crab, place it in a large pan of boiling water. Bring back to the boil, then drain and refresh. Pick the crab meat from the claws, trying not to break up the flesh too much.

Five minutes before serving, mix the fennel with the lime juice and wasabi. This will allow the flavours to infuse and break down the raw fennel.

Remove the lemongrass jelly from the refrigerator and allow to sit at room temperature for 5 minutes.

Mix the crab meat with the crème fraîche, a dash of lemon juice and coriander to taste. Season and set aside.

As you dress the plate, deep fry the soft-shell crab in the tempura batter for 3–4 minutes at 180°C.

Al's advice
Never use processed picked crab meat
– it's a poor alternative.

Duck

Terrine of duck, smoked breast, confit leg & foie gras, golden sultanas & quince purée

A tricky little terrine to build, but well worth it when presented. A lot of forward planning is required. The result is a lovely balance of textures using different cooking techniques and cuts of duck.

Serves 4

Duck Terrine

(makes 1 terrine)

500g cooked foie gras

(see basics 228)

500g duck confit

(see basics 5)

500g hot smoked duck

(see basics 19)

8 slices Parma ham

100g foie gras fat

Quince Purée

350g peeled quince

300ml red wine

100g sugar

500ml water

Garnish

golden sultanas soaked in

ruby port for 48 hours

red wine and port

reduction

(see basics 20)

Preparation

Start work on the terrine 72 hours before you want to serve it by cooking the foie gras and duck confit, following the basic recipes.

The quince purée can be made well in advance. Combine all the ingredients together and cook over a low heat for 4–5 hours (you may need to add more water). The fruit should be soft to the touch. Strain off and reserve any extra liquid. Purée the quince until smooth.

Forty-eight hours before you want to serve the terrine smoke the duck breast, following the basic recipe. Also marinate the sultanas in the ruby port.

Twenty-four hours before you want to serve the terrine, you need to start building it. (Take note, Mark Barton – not at 6.15pm on a Saturday night!)

Line a square terrine mould with cling film, then line evenly with the sliced Parma ham, allowing an overlap halfway down the sides of the terrine.

Cut the foie gras, pressed duck confit and smoked duck into six 4cm × 4cm × 12cm batons. To get a dramatic finish, you need to be very precise at this stage. Melt the foie gras fat and brush the smoked duck and duck confit batons very lightly with it. Start by placing in the smoked duck along the full length of the terrine, then add the duck confit, again making sure that the duck runs the full length of the terrine. Finally press in the foie gras batons. Repeat this process twice more, ensuring that the meat is tightly and evenly spaced and that you use alternate cuts each time. Once you have reached the top of the terrine, fold over the Parma ham. Place the terrine in the refrigerator and press for 24 hours.

Slice the terrine and allow to sit at room temperature for 5 minutes before serving

Al's advice

In making this terrine there is a certain element of "waste". Place all the offcuts of foie gras, duck confit and smoked duck in a food processor and blitz away, adding a dash of sherry vinegar. Serve on toasted brioche as a canapé.

Sandwich

Foie gras & pain d'épice sandwich, smoked duck, spiced fig & griottine cherries

A take on a classic sandwich – meat and two slices of bread.

Serves 4

Foie Gras

4 x 100g paves cooked

foie gras (see basics 228)

Pain d'Epice

8 slices pain d'épice

(see basics 211)

Smoked Duck

4 slices hot smoked duck

(see basics 19)

Garnish

4 spiced figs

(see basics 47)

12 griottine cherries

12 pieces pissant leaf

12 batons red chicory

pea shoots

beetroot cress

hazelnut vinaigrette

(see basics 27)

Preparation

Start preparing the dish 72 hours before you want to serve it by cooking the foie gras and pain d'épice, following the basic recipes.

When the pain d'épice has cooled, allow it to rest overnight at room temperature. Once it has dried out a little, slice the pain d'épice very thinly on a meat slicer, then cut it into 8cm × 4cm panels. Place on a baking sheet and put in a low oven (50°C) for 48 hours, until dry and brittle.

Cook the smoked duck and spiced figs, following the basic recipes, 24 hours before you want to serve the dish.

To finish, season the foie gras, and place the sliced smoked duck, sliced figs and cherries on top. Add the spiced bread, salads and cresses, drizzle with dressing and serve immediately.

37

Al's advice
Cooked foie gras is always best when it is allowed to sit at room temperature for 10 minutes before serving. Assemble the pain d'épice wafers at the last minute.

Sashimi

Marinated scallops, tuna & salmon, pickled radish, sesame oil & soy dressing

Sashimi is an excellent source of protein, omega-3 fats and many other nutrients such as B vitamins, selenium, magnesium and phosphorus.

Serves 4

Fish Selection

200g marinated salmon

(see basics 50)

10g sea salt

10 black peppercorns

16 coriander seeds, crushed

juice of 1 lime

4 x 75g pieces tuna loin

light soy sauce

4 large hand-dived scallops

wasabi paste

Pickled White Radish

12 x 10cm x 3cm strips white radish

500ml water

100ml rice vinegar

35g salt

35g sugar

Sesame Dressing

(see basics 51)

Garnish

20g oscietra caviar

20g trout eggs

pea shoots

coriander cress

shiso cress

Preparation

The marinated salmon should be prepared 24 hours before serving.

To pickle the radish, bring the water, vinegar, salt and sugar up to the boil, add the radish strips and simmer for 10–15 minutes until the radish is tender. Set aside and allow to cool.

Mix together the sea salt, black peppercorns, coriander seeds and lime juice. Roll the tuna loin in the sea salt mixture and allow to marinate for 20 minutes. Sear in a hot pan for 40 seconds, turning four times to ensure even cooking, then deglaze the pan with a dash of soy sauce and a squeeze of lime juice. Remove the tuna from the pan and allow to rest.

To finish the scallops, cut them into four even slices. Rub the scallop meat with a touch of wasabi paste, add a squeeze of lime juice and a few grains of salt, and allow to marinate for 10 minutes before serving.

Slice the salmon and tuna thinly. Garnish the sashimi with the caviar and trout eggs, and serve.

Hot Foie Gras

Pan-fried foie gras, endive & orange jam, roast endive, carrot & vanilla purée

Pan-fried foie gras has a unique texture and flavour. It is crucial to deglaze the foie gras with some top-quality xeres vinegar as you need the acidity to cut the richness of the foie gras. The endive jam and carrot purée give a nice balanced sweet-and-sour effect to the overall dish.

Serves 4

Foie Gras

4 x 150g slices foie gras

xeres vinegar

Belgian Endive Jam

(see basics 52)

Carrot & Vanilla Purée

(see basics 53)

Garnish

dried orange slices

(see basics 55)

braised endive

(see basics 54)

orange powder

(see basics 56)

Preparation

A very simple dish to prepare and serve. Start work 24 hours in advance by making the dried orange slices.

Using the outer leaves of the endive for the jam, make the endive jam, braised endive and carrot and vanilla purée, following the basic recipes.

Slice the whole braised endive in two lengthways. Caramelise in a little olive oil and butter until golden brown, then season and set aside. Warm the endive jam and carrot purée.

To cook the foie gras, place a non-stick pan over a medium heat. Add the foie gras and increase the temperature. Season and turn when golden brown. At this stage pour off any excess fat. Place the pan under a medium grill and continue to cook until the foie gras is soft to the touch. Season, and deglaze the pan with a dash of xeres vinegar.

Serve immediately.

Al's advice
The foie gras can be seared in advance and reheated under a hot grill.

Langoustine

Cannelloni of Scottish langoustine & lobster, baby leeks, Perigord truffle cream

Creel-caught langoustines are a joy to work with. Individually packed in tubes and flown down overnight from Scotland, they arrive at my back door alive and kicking.

Serves 4

Lobster Cannelloni

300g lobster mousse

(see basics 58)

12 pieces blanched

cannelloni pasta

Langoustine

12 large langoustines

15ml white truffle oil

lemon juice

Perigord Truffle Cream

Sauce

(see basics 76)

Garnish

4 ribbons large leek,

blanched

12 baby leeks, blanched

vegetable emulsion

(see basics 59)

12 slices Perigord truffle

picked chervil

12 baby leeks, blanched

Preparation

Lobster, langoustine and truffle – how expensive a shopping list do you want?

Start the day by making the lobster mousse, following the basic recipe. Allow 3–4 hours for the mousse to firm up in the refrigerator.

The truffle cream sauce can be made, following the basic recipe, 2–3 days in advance.

To cook and assemble the dish, blanch the pasta and refresh. Dry thoroughly and three-quarters fill with the lobster mousse. Steam for 2–3 minutes – don't get it too hot or the mousse will soufflé!

Grill the langoustines under a medium grill with a dash of truffle oil and a touch of lemon juice, and season.

Gently warm the truffle cream sauce. Do not boil the sauce or it will loose its amazing aroma and flavour.

Reheat the leek ribbons and baby leeks in the emulsion, then dry on kitchen paper.

Assemble the dish at the last minute.

Note

This dish is near on impossible to do at home as it will not be easy for you to find Perigord truffles, live langoustines and live native lobsters down at your local supermarket. This is the type of dish you go to restaurants to eat.

Goat's Cheese

Goat's cheese fondue, poached pear, gingerbread, white truffle honey & port reduction

Lower in fat than cow's cheese, goat's cheese is an excellent source of protein and calcium. Calcium is well known for supporting the density and strength of bones.

Serves 4

Goat's Cheese Fondue

100g Saint Maure

100g Crottin Chavignol

75g crème fraîche

Gingerbread

24 slices dried gingerbread

(see basics 212)

Garnish

12 slices red wine poached

pear (see basics 49)

red wine and port

reduction

(see basics 20)

white truffle honey

(see basics 48)

mixed cress

12 pieces pissant leaf

Preparation

Start by making the gingerbread, following the basic recipe. Allow to cool overnight then slice very finely and evenly on a meat slicer. Allow to dry in a low oven (50°C) overnight.

The red wine reduction, truffle honey and poached pears can all be prepared 24 hours in advance.

To make the goat's cheese fondue, let the Saint Maure and Crottin Chavignol sit at room temperature for 1 hour. Blend the cheeses until smooth then add the crème fraîche. Place in the refrigerator for 6 hours before serving.

Assemble the goat's cheese and gingerbread at the last minute.

45

Al's advice
If you prefer, you can replace the
goat's cheese with a nice creamy
blue cheese such as bleu d'Auvergne.

'Les truffe.'
'How much a kilo?'
'Are you are having a laugh, Carlos?'
'Okay, give me 8 kilos of your finest.'

Lobster

Poached lobster with Russian salad

Lobster is an excellent source of protein, vitamins and minerals. It is low in saturated fat and brings the healthy benefits of omega-3 fatty acids.

Serves 4

Lobster

2 native lobsters,

approx. 750g each

1 court bouillon

(see basics 60)

Russian Salad

150g diced carrot,

150g diced potato

100g fresh peas

100g chopped

haricots verts

100g fresh mayonnaise

(see basics 61)

50g marinated anchovy

Lobster Dressing

(see basics 62)

Garnish

picked chervil

picked chive tips

dried lobster coral

(see basics 64)

blanched lobster head

Preparation

Make the court bouillon 24 hours in advance and allow to infuse in the refrigerator.

There is debate regarding the best way to kill/cook lobsters – my own preferred method is to quickly despatch the lobster with a large sharp knife through the head, then cook straight away.

Bring the court bouillon to the boil, add the lobsters and simmer for 8 minutes. Remove the lobsters from the bouillon and allow to cool.

When the lobsters have cooled, shell them and set the meat aside. Keep the lobster carcasses to make the lobster dressing, following the basic recipe.

Blanch and refresh the carrot, potato, peas and haricots verts separately. Drain well and place on a kitchen cloth to ensure that they are all as dry as possible.

Mix the vegetables with the mayonnaise and anchovy, and season to taste. The Russian salad will lose its freshness if it is made up too far in advance, so prepare it at the last minute.

Al's advice

Avoid the cheaper and inferior Canadian lobster. It is easy to identify because of its slightly orange and blue colour when alive. Native lobsters are such a beautiful dark blue that they are almost black.

49

Oysters

Oyster panna cotta, hot oyster beignet, red wine shallots & caviar dressing

By using a light tempura batter on the oysters, you change their texture and flavour. Purists would cringe, so please feel free to garnish the dish as suggested and serve raw fresh oysters as nature intended.

Serves 4

Oyster Panna Cotta

(see basics 63)

Red Wine Shallots

(see basics 204)

Caviar Dressing

(see basics 231)

Garnish

tempura batter

(see basics 22)

12 native oysters, shelled

rock salt

lemon juice

12 pieces blanched sliced

cucumber

Preparation

Simple preparation and stunning flavours and textures!

The panna cotta is best made on the day you wish to serve it. Oysters are superb when they are fresh from the shell, but break down quickly when prepared.

The red wine shallots will keep for 2–3 weeks in a sealed jar in the refrigerator.

Caviar dressing is a very expensive garnish to prepare. But don't skimp on the caviar – you want to be able to taste it.

Finish the dish by making the batter, following the basic recipe. Deep fry the native oysters at 190°C for 2–3 minutes, and season with rock salt and lemon juice. Dress the plate with the blanched cucumber, caviar dressing and panna cotta, add the tempura oysters and serve.

Al's advice
When shelling the oysters, shuck then pour the oyster and juice into a fine sieve, reserving the juices on one side. Gently wash the oysters under cold running water. Return them to the strained juices and place in the refrigerator. This technique for oysters may be frowned upon but it ensures that no broken shell or grit makes its way from the oyster into your mouth. By returning the oyster to its own juices you ensure that it retains its natural flavour.

Roast Chicken

Roast chicken terrine with garlic & shallots

Think roast Sunday lunch and all its glorious flavours. One of chef Will Holland's creations and a great starter. Will also convinced me to like bread sauce after tasting his recipe.

Serves 10

Chicken Terrine

(makes 1 terrine)

2 x 1.75kg free-range

chickens from Loué

olive oil

8 banana shallots

4 whole heads garlic

thyme

rosemary

bay leaf

4 red peppers

8 slices Parma ham

Dijon mustard

Bread Sauce

(see basics 67)

Garnish

pickled shallots

(see basics 36)

red wine dressing

(see basics 68)

picked pea shoots

and cress

Preparation

This terrine is best made the day before you would like to serve it.

The basic recipes – bread sauce, pickled shallots and red wine dressing – can all be made in advance.

Place the chickens in a roasting tin. Add olive oil, the shallots, garlic cloves and herbs, and season well. Put in the oven at 200°C for 50 minutes, basting every 10 minutes. Remove from the oven and allow to cool for 45 minutes.

Put the red peppers under a hot grill, turning every 2 minutes until the skins are black all over. Place in a bowl and cover with cling film. When cool, peel off the skins and deseed and quarter the peppers. Season and set aside.

Line a triangular terrine with cling film. Line the base and sides with the Parma ham, allowing a good overlap of ham.

Break down the chicken, trying to keep the meat in nice large pieces. Place it in a large bowl and add some of the roasting juices and Dijon mustard to taste. Peel the garlic cloves. Build the terrine while the meat and vegetables are still warm, alternating layers of chicken, red pepper and shallots/garlic until you reach the top of the terrine. Fold over the ham and place the terrine in the refrigerator for 12 hours. Press gently.

Slice the terrine and allow it to sit at room temperature for 10 minutes before serving.

Al's advice
The chicken can be replaced with guinea fowl, pheasant or poussin to achieve a similar end result.

Scallops

Roast scallops, cauliflower purée & beignet, smoked bacon & curry oil

This dish is one of the few that remain from my first ever à la carte menu at the restaurant. The combination of scallop, cauliflower and curry just works so well. We use only hand-dived scallops from the north-west coast of Scotland. They arrive with us less than 24 hours after leaving the sea and are often still pulsing as we cook them.

Serves 4

Scallops

12 large hand-dived

scallops

50ml olive oil

25g unsalted butter

lemon juice to taste

Curry Tempura Batter

(see basics 23)

16 cauliflower florets,

blanched

cauliflower purée

(see basics 16)

Curry Oil

(see basics 17)

Garnish

bacon powder

(see basics 15)

cayenne pepper

black onion seeds

red pepper powder

8 dried smoked back

bacon crisps

(see basics 15)

Preparation

The freshness and quality of the scallops is the key to this very simple and effective dish. Soaked scallops in tubs are an option not worth using.

All the basics recipe can be prepared the day before.

To finish and serve the dish, make the curry tempura batter and deep fry the cauliflower florets at 190°C for 2–3 minutes until golden brown and crispy. Season and set aside. Warm the cauliflower purée.

Sauté the scallops in the olive oil in a hot non-stick pan for 1 minute on one side, until golden brown. Season and turn. Add the butter, season and continue to cook, basting the scallops, for a further minute. Add a dash of lemon juice and rest for $1^1/_2$ minutes. Serve straight away.

Al's advice
You could replace the cauliflower
purée with butternut squash or
parsnip

Smoked Salmon

Organic smoked salmon, native oysters, pickled seaweed & oscietra caviar

Smoked salmon is great for the diet-conscious, being high in good fats, low in saturated fat, high in protein and minerals yet almost completely carbohydrate free.

Serves 4

Smoked Salmon & Oysters

12 medium native oysters

4 large slices

oak-smoked salmon

Pickled Seaweeds

wakame seaweed

hijiki seaweed

100ml white wine vinegar

100ml water

50g sugar

salt to taste

Oyster Vinaigrette

(see basics 26)

Garnish

12 lime segments

50g oscietra caviar

pea shoots

Preparation

Pickling the seaweed is best done a minimum of 24 hours in advance.

Warm up the vinegar and water, add the sugar and whisk until dissolved. Season and pour onto the dried seaweeds (keep them separate). Allow to soak overnight.

The dressing is best prepared 2–3 hours before serving as the vinegar breaks down the oysters and loses its freshness.

Wrap the oysters in the smoked salmon 30 minutes before serving. If you prefer the oysters slightly cured, you could wrap them in the smoked salmon 2 hours before serving. The salt in the salmon will start to cure the oysters.

Dress and finish the dish at the last minute and serve immediately.

57

Al's advice
Opinion is divided among chefs as to whether native or rock oysters are the best. I love both. So it's your call.

Tomato

Pressed tomato terrine, tomato jelly, Picadon goat's cheese & Bloody Mary sorbet

A dish that really catches the essence of the summer. Wait until May or June before using tomato as the main ingredient in a dish – the flavour will have increased and the acidity reduced, giving a much better result all round. When possible buy tomatoes that have been ripened on the vine. This dish also works well with the addition of some poached lobster or langoustine.

Serves 10

Tomato Consommé

(see basics 31)

3 leaves gelatine per

500ml liquid (you need

500ml for four servings)

Bloody Mary Sorbet

(see basics 35)

Tomato Terrine

(makes 1 terrine)

24 large plum vine

tomatoes

salt and pepper to taste

75ml eight-year-old

balsamic vinegar

Goat's Cheese Fondue

100g Picadon goat's

cheese

50g crème fraîche

25ml double cream

Garnish

extra virgin olive oil

sprigs of basil cress

dried basil crisps

Preparation

Make the tomato consommé and Bloody Mary base 24 hours in advance.

To make the terrine, blanch the tomatoes and refresh. Peel, deseed and cut into petals. Place on kitchen paper to remove excess moisture. Season the tomato petals well and add the balsamic vinegar. Line a small triangular terrine mould with cling film and layer in the tomato petals. Press with a 5kg (minimum) weight overnight.

The goat's cheese fondue can be made well in advance. Blend the goat's cheese and crème fraîche until smooth. Add the cream and season then place in the refrigerator to firm up. Quenelle and place back in the refrigerator 1 hour before required.

To set the jelly and finish the dish, soak the gelatine in cold water until soft. Heat 100ml of the consommé and whisk in the gelatine, then return to 400ml of the chilled consommé. Set in four large serving bowls for 1 hour before serving.

Al's advice
Don't keep the tomato
consommé in a metal bowl
or dish as the metal
can taint the delicate
flavour

59

Tuna
Salad of yellowfin tuna 'Niçoise'

Tuna and anchovies are both excellent in providing omega-3 essential fatty acids which help to metabolise 'bad fats' in the body. Tuna is also a rich source of protein, B vitamins and many important minerals such as selenium and magnesium.

Serves 4

Tuna

4 x 150g yellow fin

tuna loin batons

sea salt

ground black pepper

50ml olive oil

light soy sauce

lime juice

Lemon Oil Dressing

(see basics 38)

Garnish

24 black olive slices

12 marinated anchovy fillets

24 pieces tomato

concassée

split haricots verts

4 softly boiled quail's eggs

8 slices cooked ratte potato

picked basil cress

Preparation

Tuna loin freezes very well. My advice would be to buy a largish piece of tuna (1–2kg), portion it, wrap it in cling film and freeze. It can then be used as required.

Marinate the tuna loin in the sea salt and black pepper for 2 hours before serving.

All other basic jobs and preparation can be done in advance.

To cook and serve the tuna, get a non-stick pan very hot and sear the tuna for 45 seconds, turning four times to ensure even cooking. Remove from the heat and deglaze the pan with a dash of light soy sauce and a squeeze of lime juice. Do not add any additional seasoning as the marinade and the soy sauce both contain a lot of salt.

Slice and serve.

Al's advice
Rare tuna only, please! Tuna has a very low fat content and will be dry if cooked too far.

Jerusalem Artichoke

Jerusalem artichoke & Perigord truffle risotto, white truffle & artichoke velouté

When it comes to truffles, the famous Perigord variety are the cream of the crop. The arrival of the first kilo always brings a ripple of excitement around the boys in the kitchen. Look for pungent aroma, firmness to the touch and black flesh with good marbling. Also remember that there is no such thing as a cheap truffle – as with all things in life, you get what you pay for.

Serves 4

Risotto Rice

50g shallot brunoise

25g garlic purée

100g butter

150g arborio risotto rice

100ml dry white wine

450ml vegetable nage
(see basics 11)

75g Jerusalem
artichoke purée
(see basics 73)

50g crème fraîche

50g Parmesan cheese

White Truffle & Artichoke

Velouté

200g Jerusalem
artichoke purée
(see basics 73)

100ml steamed milk

20ml white truffle oil

lemon juice, to taste

Garnish

12 cooked poivrade baby
artichokes (see basics 74)

50 slices fresh Perigord truffle

100g picked pea shoots

Preparation

To make the risotto, sweat the shallots and garlic purée in the butter. Cook for 4–5 minutes without colouring. Stir in the risotto rice and cook for a further 2 minutes. Add the white wine and reduce by half. Add half the vegetable nage and simmer over a gentle heat for 12 minutes, adding more nage as required. Remove from the heat when the rice still has a little bite. Pour onto a tray and spread out to allow the rice to cool evenly. Cover with cling film and set aside.

To finish the dish, gently heat the cooked risotto, adding the artichoke purée. Cook for 3–4 minutes, until the rice is tender, then add the crème fraîche and Parmesan and season to taste.

For the artichoke velouté, heat the purée and add the steamed milk and truffle oil. Season and add the lemon juice.

Spoon the risotto rice into large metal rings. Carefully remove the rings, add the artichokes and sauce, then top with copious amounts of sliced truffle.

63

Al's advice
It's always a good idea to cook
the risotto rice in advance. You
can control the texture and
consistency. This allows you to
concentrate on other things
while you're assembling
the dish.

Salmon

Ballotine of salmon, horseradish & potato mousse, beetroot purée

Salmon is wonderfully rich in omega-3 essential fatty acids. EFAs promote a healthy cardiovascular system and immune system and are known to relieve the symptoms of depression. Salmon is low in saturated fat and calories and is an excellent source of protein.

Serves 4

Salmon Ballotine

450g organic salmon fillet, with no skin, bone or blood line (reserve the skin)

Horseradish & Potato Mousse

(see basics 28)

Horseradish Relish

(see basics 75)

Garnish

dried salmon skin

(see basics 18)

beetroot purée

(see basics 40)

salmon eggs

baby sorrel

Preparation

Cut the salmon into two strips approximately 15cm long. Season well and place one on top of the other. Wrap well in cling film to form a long, tightly packed sausage. Cook in a water bath or bain-marie at 45°C for 1 hour. Refresh in iced water and allow to set overnight.

All the other basics can be made 12 hours in advance.

To dry the salmon skin, make sure it is free from any salmon flesh. Cover a baking sheet with greaseproof paper and brush with olive oil. Place the salmon skin on the paper scales side down, brush with olive oil and season again. Cover with another sheet of greaseproof paper and place another baking sheet on top. Put in the oven at 160°C for 15–20 minutes until the skin is dry and crispy. Cut into strips while the skin is still warm. You *must* keep the scales on the fish skin to get the right result.

Al's advice
Organic salmon is an essential part of the dish. The cheaper farmed alternative has received much bad press recently, in my opinion quite rightly.

65

'Beautiful fresh ingredients
are key when producing
any dish, as the end result
will only ever be as good
as what you have
put into it.'

Chef John Burton Race

mains
2

Coq

Coq au vin, braised corn-fed chicken in red wine and tarragon, pomme purée, roast shallots & cèpe fricassée

A classic dish that is hard to beat. It is very important to make sure that the chicken you buy is of the best quality, preferably corn-fed. I suggest using traditional free-range chicken from Loué in south-west France.

Serves 4

Chicken

1 x 1.5kg corn-fed Loué

chicken

750ml red wine

2 heads garlic

2 sprigs thyme

2 bay leaves

600ml brown chicken stock

(see basics 2)

600ml white chicken stock

(see basics 1)

150g unsalted butter

Garnish

pomme purée

(see basics 66)

12 roast shallots

200g bouchon cèpes

100g unsalted butter

5g chopped garlic

12 pieces confit tomato

(see basics 45)

dried tarragon

(see basics 69)

50g chopped tarragon

Preparation

Portion the chicken by removing the legs and splitting the drumsticks from the thighs. Split the crown into four even pieces.

Marinate the chicken in the red wine, garlic, thyme and bay leaves for 24 hours in the refrigerator.

Strain the red wine, garlic and herbs and add to the chicken stocks. Dry the chicken thoroughly on kitchen paper. Caramelise the chicken in the butter – it should be golden brown all over.

Place the chicken in a casserole dish and cover with the red wine and chicken stock. Bring to the boil and skim. Place the casserole dish in the oven at 150°C and cook for 60 minutes. Remove from the oven and allow to cool for 30 minutes, then strain off the stock into a pan and reduce quickly by two-thirds. Correct the seasoning and pour over the cooked chicken.

While the chicken is cooking, prepare the pomme purée and roast the shallots.

Beef

Roast côte de bœuf, wild garlic, confit shallots & roast garlic

The maturation and ageing of the beef is the key to the flavour and tenderness of this dish – a minimum of 21 days' hanging, and longer if possible. Try to source select Aberdeen Angus beef.

Serves 4

Côte de Bœuf

2 x 400g beef cutlets

50ml olive oil

100g unsalted butter

2 cloves garlic, crushed.

thyme and bay leaf

Roast Garlic

4 heads new season garlic

unsalted butter

Confit Shallots

(see basics 106)

xeres vinegar

Béarnaise Sauce

(see basics 105)

Red Wine Sauce

(see basics 33)

Garnish

24 pieces fresh wild garlic

picked watercress

Preparation

Start by sealing the beef. In a large sauté pan, colour the beef evenly in the olive oil, ensuring that it is nicely browned. This should take about 10 minutes. Season well, and add the butter, garlic and herbs. To cook medium rare, place in the oven at 200°C for 25–30 minutes, basting every 10 minutes with the foaming butter. Allow 30 minutes' resting time.

The garnish is all very straightforward. Cut the garlic in half and place in a pan of cold water. Bring to the boil then refresh; repeat this process three times. To finish, caramelise in foaming butter.

Confit shallots can be browned in a little duck fat until golden brown. Deglaze with a dash of sherry vinegar.

The wild garlic can be lightly sautéed in a little olive oil at the last minute.

Serve with classic Béarnaise and red wine sauces.

Al's advice
Cooking times can vary greatly on all meat cuts. A temperature probe as a guide will help with consistency.

73

Bouillabaisse

Sea bass, red mullet, gilthead bream, John Dory & baby squid, bouillabaisse broth, saffron potato & baby fennel

Serves 4

sea bass, red mullet, bream,
John Dory. 12 pieces baby
squid tentacles
(allow 150–200g
fish per person)

Bouillabaisse Marinade
(see basics 43)

Bouillabaisse Broth
1kg fish bones
1kg fresh gurnard
1 head fennel
1 head garlic
150ml olive oil
large pinch of saffron
thyme
3 star anise
750ml dry white wine
100ml Pernod
500g tomato fondue
(see basics 7)
1 litre fish stock
(see basics 9)
salt
lemon juice

Garnish
12 pieces baby fennel,
blanched
12 pieces saffron new potatoes
(see basics 78)

Options
crusty French bread
rouille (see basics 79)

Preparation

Start by preparing the fish. All the fish should be scaled, filleted and pin-boned; keep all the bones for the broth. Marinate the fish for 3 hours in the refrigerator.

Roughly chop the fish bones, gurnard, fennel and garlic. Sauté in a large stock pot with the olive oil until golden brown. Remove 25% of the bones to refresh the broth at a later stage. Add the saffron, thyme, star anise, white wine and Pernod to the bones, and reduce by half. Add the tomato fondue and cook gently for 5 minutes. Add the fish stock, bring to the boil, skim and cook quickly for 20 minutes. Pass through a coarse sieve and return to the heat, adding the reserved fish bones. Cook for a further 5 minutes, then blend. Pass through a fine sieve and season with salt, lemon juice and a dash of Pernod.

Blanch the baby fennel. Cook the saffron potatoes, strain and keep warm.

To finish the dish, gently heat the broth, making sure that it does not boil. Add the marinated fish fillets and baby fennel and poach gently for 4–5 minutes.

At home, serve crusty French bread and rouille on the side.

Al's advice
A short cooking time on the broth will
guarantee freshness and flavour.

Bream

Fillet of bream, pak choi, wild mushrooms, Vietnamese-style broth with citronella & crisp shallots

Bream contains omega-3 and is also a good source of protein. The rich phytonutrient content of pak choi increases antioxidant levels in the body, protecting our cells from free radical damage.

Serves 4

*2 x 500g gilthead bream,
scaled, filleted and
pin-boned*

Broth

*750ml white chicken stock
(see basics 1)
55ml light soy sauce
50ml Thai fish sauce
100g fresh ginger
10 sticks fresh lemongrass
1 bunch fresh coriander
1 red chilli
1 lime*

Garnish

*crispy shallots
(see basics 80)
2 heads pak choi,
cut in half
batons of red chilli
400g mixed mushrooms
(enoki, pholio, shiitake,
oyster)
1 bunch spring onions,
finely sliced
coriander cress*

Preparation

This is one of the easier dishes in this book to prepare and serve, and it is also one of the healthiest. The idea for the dish came while I was travelling with my family in Vietnam.

Make the broth by bringing the chicken stock and other ingredients to the boil. Allow to simmer for 5 minutes, then remove from the heat and allow to infuse for 1 hour. Strain through a sieve.

Prepare the crispy shallots, following the basic recipe.

To finish the dish, bring the broth to the boil and poach the pak choi for 3 minutes. Add the fish fillets, chilli and mushrooms, and simmer for 3 minutes. Correct seasoning and serve, finishing at the last minute with the crispy shallots, spring onions and coriander cress

Al's advice
A welcome addition could be some
cooked chicken pieces. Chicken
stock could be replaced with fish
stock for our non-meat-eating friends!

Mallard

Ballotine of wild duck & foie gras, endive salad, endive confit with thyme, roast endive, cherry & kirsch sauce

Cooking time on this dish is critical: too much and the mallard overcooks and the foie gras breaks down; not enough and the foie gras will be cold.

Serves 4

Braised Mallard Legs

4 mallard legs

olive oil

200ml red wine

250ml duck stock

(see basics 205)

thyme and bay leaf

2 garlic cloves

Mallard Ballotine

4 mallard breasts

4 x 75g pan-fried foie gras

pain d'épice crumb

flour, egg, breadcrumbs

100g unsalted butter.

Duck Cherry Sauce

(see basics 206)

Garnish

4 cider fondant potatoes

(see basics 84)

12 pieces braised chicory

(see basics 207)

160g chicory jam

(see basics 85)

4 chicory salads

hazelnut vinaigrette

(see basics 27)

4 thyme sprigs

Preparation

The first job is to caramelise the mallard legs in a little olive oil until golden brown. Next reduce the red wine by half and add to the duck stock with the thyme, bay leaf and garlic. Add the duck legs and braise in a low oven at 120–130°C for 2 hours.

Remove the skin from the mallard breasts. Butterfly the breasts and tenderise with a meat hammer until the meat is even in thickness. Roll the cold pan-fried foie gras in the pan d'épice crumb. Wrap the mallard breasts around the foie gras, ensuring that the meat covers the foie gras completely. Pané at the last minute.

Cider fondant potatoes, braised chicory and chicory jam can all be made on the day. Chicory salad needs to be prepared at last minute.

Cook the mallard ballotine by making a beurre noisette. Colour the mallard evenly until golden brown – this should take 4–5 minutes. Rest in a warm place for 5 minutes.

Reheat the braised legs and garnish. Dress the chicory salads at the last minute with the hazelnut dressing and serve immediately.

Al's advice
The same cooking technique can be applied to any type of duck.

Oxtail

Ballotine of oxtail with smoked bacon & shallots, horseradish pomme purée & horseradish cream

A stunning autumn/winter dish, probably on the menus of many of the chefs who have been through the kitchen at Le Manoir aux Quat'Saisons. This is rich, delicious comfort food, just as Monsieur Blanc intended.

Serves 4

Oxtail
1 x 2.5kg whole oxtail
4 blanched
cabbage leaves
8 roast shallots
8 pieces smoked bacon
200g wild mushrooms
300g unsalted butter
diced carrot, onion, garlic,
celery, thyme and bay leaf
500ml red wine
500ml brown chicken stock
(see basics 2)
500ml veal stock
(see basics 3)

Horseradish Cream
(see basics 29)

Horseradish Pomme Purée
(see basics 92)

Sauce
10% of the roasted bones
oxtail braising liquor
thyme and bay leaf
100ml red wine
15ml red wine vinegar
250g sliced button
mushrooms

Garnish
20 pieces roast cèpes
20 bacon lardons
20 pieces roast baby onion
fried parsley
(see basics 93)

Preparation

To bone the oxtail, take a small sharp knife and slice along the underside. Carefully peel back the flesh until you reach the middle of the other side (it is easier to do one side, then repeat the process on the other), taking as much meat as possible off the bone while trying at all times to keep the outer skin intact. Reserve the bone.

Place the boned tail skin side down and line with the blanched cabbage leaves, then place in the roast shallots, smoked bacon and mushrooms. Roll the cabbage leaves over the stuffing to create a sealed unit, then overlap the oxtail to encompass the farce. Tie tightly with butcher's string.

To make the braising liquor, chop the oxtail bone and place in a deep roasting tin. Caramelise in 150g of the butter until golden brown. Remove 10% of the bones to refresh the sauce later. Add the mixed vegetables and herbs and cook out for a further 5 minutes, then pour off the excess fat. Add the red wine and reduce the liquid by half. Add the stocks, bring to the boil and skim.

Caramelise the boned and stuffed oxtail in the remaining 150g butter. Start over quite a high heat, then reduce the heat and cook to achieve a dark golden brown colour. Place the oxtail in the braising liquor and cook in the oven at 130°C for about 4 hours. The meat should be tender and soft to touch. Remove the oxtail from the liquor carefully and set aside to cool. When cold, carefully remove the string. Roll the oxtail tightly in cling film and place in the refrigerator overnight.

To make the sauce, strain the braising liquor through a fine sieve. Reduce by two-thirds. Add the reserved oxtail bones, red wine, red wine vinegar and mushrooms. Bring to the boil, skim and simmer for 20–30 minutes. Pass through a fine sieve and correct seasoning.

To serve the dish, cut the oxtail into four large pieces, add 100ml of the sauce and a touch of chicken stock and reheat in a medium oven, basting often, for 25–30 minutes.

Al's advice
Boning and rolling the oxtail is a very difficult job, but the end result more than justifies the effort. One of my all-time favourite dishes to eat.

Rabbit

Roast saddle, pan-fried rack, braised shoulder, liver &
kidney of rabbit, lettuce ravioli, pea & carrot purée, rabbit jus

Serves 4

*2 x 1.5kg French farmed
rabbits (the rabbit should be
broken down to best end,
shoulders, saddle/loin, legs
and the offal)*

Rabbit Shoulder

*4 rabbit shoulders
100ml red wine
thyme and bay leaf
160g rabbit farce
(see basics 195)
red rabbit sauce
(see basics 199)*

Rabbit Loin (saddle meat)

*4 x 80g pieces rabbit loin
50g herb butter
(see basics 200)
50ml olive oil
25g unsalted butter*

Rabbit Ravioli

*1 confit rabbit leg
(see basics 197)
160g chicken mousse
(see basics 87)
25g mustard seeds
chopped chervil, tarragon
and chives
8 flat lettuce leaves,
blanched*

Rabbit Best End

*4 x 30g rabbit best ends,
French-trimmed
Dijon mustard
soft herb crust (see basics 6)*

Rabbit Sauces

*red rabbit sauce
(see basics 199)
mustard seed sauce
(see basics 198)*

Garnish

*4 pieces rabbit liver
4 pieces rabbit kidney
200g pea purée
(see basics 190)
200g carrot purée
(see basics 196)
12 baby carrots
blanched haricots verts*

Preparation

The first little job is to butcher the rabbit as specified. Keep all the bones to make the rabbit sauces.

Bone out the shoulders and marinate in the red wine, thyme and bay leaf for 8 hours. Stuff with the rabbit farce and sew up with fine string. Braise in the red rabbit sauce at 140°C for 90 minutes, until tender. Remove the rabbit shoulders from the sauce and allow to cool. Remove the string. Roll into an even ballotine, wrap in cling film and place in the refrigerator for 24 hours.

With the rabbit loin, peel back the outer skin and trim off any excess fat from the skin. Brush liberally with the herb butter, then roll the skin over the loin and tie firmly with fine string. Set aside.

For the ravioli, confit the rabbit leg 24 hours in advance and flake the meat into small strips. Make the chicken mousse and add the mustard seeds, herbs and rabbit confit. Lay four of the lettuce leaves flat and add a quarter of the mousse mixture. Place a second leaf on top and wrap around the mousse. Set aside.

Rabbit sauces and purées can all be made, following the basic recipes, 24 hours in advance.

To bring it all together, reheat the rabbit shoulder in some of the rabbit liquor in a warm oven for 25–30 minutes. Pan fry the loin in olive oil and butter over a medium heat for 3–4 minutes until golden brown. Rest for 5 minutes.

The ravioli should be steamed for 3 minutes at 100°C in a Thermomix, or steamed gently conventionally.

At the last minute, sauté the best end for 1 minute in a hot pan. Brush with Dijon mustard and dip into the herb crust.

The liver and kidneys should be seared for 30 seconds in a non-stick pan.

All sauces and purées can be heated up at the last minute.

Al's advice

One of the more complex dishes to prepare and serve. Use wild rabbit to practise the butchery skills required.

Red Mullet

Ballotine of red mullet, chorizo & black olive, saffron risotto, squid fricassée, rouille & roast red pepper mayonnaise

Serves 4

Red Mullet

2 x 500g red mullet

red mullet farce

(see basics 208)

olive oil

lemon juice

Rouille

(see basics 79)

Roast Red Pepper

Mayonnaise

(see basics 86)

Saffron Risotto

(see basics 12)

Garnish

20 pieces baby squid

tentacles

20 pieces baby squid rings

confit onions

croutons

confit tomato

(see basics 45)

basil cress

Preparation

Scale and gut the red mullet carefully. Remove the head and rinse the fish under cold water, then dry on a kitchen towel. Fillet the fish from the inside out, ensuring that the skin down the back remains intact; pin-bone and set aside. Prepare the red mullet farce and roll into two cylinders each of around 200g. Wrap the red mullet fillet around the farce then roll tightly in cling film. Place in the refrigerator for 24 hours.

Rouille and red pepper mayonnaise can also be prepared, following basic recipes, 24 hours in advance.

To finish the dish, cut the red mullet ballotines into four, then remove the cling film. Sauté in a little olive oil on both sides until golden brown. Place in the oven at 180°C for 5 minutes, basting with the olive oil. Season and add a dash of lemon juice, then allow to rest for 5 minutes.

Gently warm the risotto and season.

Sauté the squid with the confit onions and croutons. Add the tomato and basil cress at the last minute.

Venison

Loin of venison with pancetta, violet potato, spiced red cabbage, braised salsify in red wine, bitter chocolate & port sauce

Venison is an essential part of any autumn/winter – menu amazing flavour and low in fat compared with other red meats.

Serves 4

Venison Loin

400g venison loin

12 slices extra thin pancetta

50ml olive oil

75g unsalted butter

Venison Marinade

(see basics 4)

Bitter Chocolate Sauce

(see basics 154)

Garnish

12 pieces diced cooked

beetroot (see basics 39)

12 glazed salsify

(see basics 81)

300g spiced red cabbage

(see basics 21)

160g violet potato purée

(see basics 82)

glazed blackberries

(see basics 83)

deep-fried celery leaves

Preparation

Marinate the venison loin for 12 hours. Remove from the marinade and dry on kitchen paper. Do not leave it any longer or the alcohol will start to 'cook' the meat.

You can reuse the marinade three times if it is kept in the refrigerator.

The bitter chocolate sauce and all the basic vegetable garnishes can be prepared 24 hours in advance.

One hour before serving, wrap the marinated venison loin in the pancetta and tie with thin butcher's string.

Caramelise the venison loin evenly in the olive oil until golden brown. Place in the oven at 190°C for 4–5 minutes, then allow to rest for 10 minutes.

Reheat all the garnishes. Slice the venison and serve. Don't season the sliced venison with salt as the pancetta will add enough salt to the meat.

AJ's advice

We request that our butcher hangs our venison saddles for a minimum of 28 days.

Wild Boar

Braised haunch & roast best end of wild boar, chanterelle à la crème, roast root vegetables & purées, braising liquor

Marcassin and sanglier are two terms commonly used to describe wild boar. Marcassin usually refers to a beast of six months old or younger, while sanglier describes a more mature animal with a slightly stronger taste.

Serves 4

Braised Haunch
*4 x 100g pieces wild boar
haunch
100g unsalted butter
500g wild boar bones,
chopped
diced carrot, onion, celery
300ml red wine
500ml veal stock
(see basics 3)
600ml brown chicken stock
(see basics 2)
thyme and bay leaf
10 juniper berries, crushed*

Best End of Wild Boar
*500g wild boar best end,
French-trimmed
50ml olive oil
50g Dijon mustard*

Chanterelle à la Crème
(see basics 209)

Soft Herb Crust
(see basics 6)

Garnish
*12 pieces roast shallot
12 pieces butternut squash
12 parsnip cones
100g unsalted butter
parsnip purée
(see basics 94)
butternut squash purée
(see basics 95)
shallot and onion purée
(see basics 96)
curly kale
vegetable emulsion
(see basics 59)*

Preparation

Caramelise the wild boar pieces in a deep casserole dish with the butter until golden brown. Remove the meat from the butter and set aside. Add the wild boar bones and cook until dark brown – you may need to add more butter, depending on the fat content of the bones. Add the chopped vegetables and cook for a further 4–5 minutes. Strain off the excess fat, return the pan to the heat and add the red wine. Reduce by half, then add the stocks, thyme, bay and juniper. Bring to the boil, skim and simmer for 1 hour.

Add the caramelised wild boar haunch and place in the oven at 140°C for 2–3 hours, until the meat is tender. Carefully remove the haunch. Strain the liquor through a fine sieve and reduce quickly to a sauce consistency. Set aside.

All other basics and vegetables can be prepared 24 hours in advance.

To cook and serve the best end, sauté the French-trimmed boar, fat side down, in the olive oil over a medium heat. Cook until the fat is rendered down – this should take 4–5 minutes. Turn over and place in the oven at 180°C for 6–8 minutes, then remove from the pan and rest for 10 minutes. When rested, brush the meat liberally with the Dijon mustard, add a tablespoon of the chanterelle à la crème and coat in the herb crust. To serve, place back in the oven for 6 minutes at 180°C.

To reheat the braised meat, add 75ml of the reduced braising liquor and a touch of water and place in the oven at 180°C for 15 minutes, basting it with its own juices.

Al's advice

Wood Pigeon

Grilled breast of wood pigeon, fresh herb macaroni, curly kale, celeriac cream & red wine sauce

Like all game birds, wood pigeon contain very little natural fat. A gentle cooking method is required. Grilling the wood pigeon breasts in cream is a technique that was first shown to me by John Burton Race.

Serves 4

Pigeon Breasts

8 wood pigeon breasts, skin removed

Marinade

100ml olive oil

1 sprig rosemary

1 sprig thyme

12 black peppercorns

4 cloves garlic, crushed

6 juniper berries, crushed

Cooking Liquor

100ml double cream

50g unsalted butter

1 sprig thyme

2 bay leaves

1 clove garlic, crushed

Fresh Herb Macaroni

160g herb purée
(see basics 77)

12 pieces macaroni pasta, blanched

Gruyère gratin
(see basics 213)

celeriac cream
(see basics 184)

Garnish

curly kale, blanched and refreshed

vegetable emulsion
(see basics 59)

red wine sauce
(see basics 33)

deep-fried celery leaf

Preparation

Trim the pigeon breasts to remove any remaining skin or fat. Place in the marinade, cover and put in the refrigerator for a maximum of 24 hours. The marinade can be reused.

The herb purée should be piped into the blanched macaroni pasta and put back in the refrigerator.

The garnish and basic recipes can all be prepared 24 hours in advance.

To cook the pigeon, put the breasts in a casserole dish and pour over the cream. Add the butter, thyme, bay leaf and crushed garlic. Place the dish under a preheated medium grill for 4–5 minutes, basting with the cream. Allow to rest for 5 minutes. The pigeon breast should always be served rare.

While the pigeon is resting, reheat the macaroni by topping with the Gruyère gratin and placing under the grill for 5 minutes. At the last minute, heat the kale in the emulsion for 2 minutes.

Al's advice
This cooking method can also be applied to partridge or pheasant

Woodcock

Roast woodcock with foie gras & boudin noir, cider fondant potato, braised chestnuts & Brussels sprouts, Pedro Ximenez sauce

Roast woodcock has always traditionally been served with the head as part of the garnish. The head would be split open, after snapping off the beak. You would then use the beak as a little spoon to enjoy the treats inside. Nice.

Serves 4

Woodcock

4 x 150g fresh woodcock

100g unsalted butter

4 x 75g slices foie gras

xeres vinegar

Pedro Ximenez Sauce

(see basics 89)

Garnish

16 pieces glazed chestnuts

(see basics 90)

16 Brussels sprouts

16 slices boudin noir

200g champ

(see basics 91)

deep-fried celery leaves

4 cider fondant potatoes

(see basics 84)

Preparation

The most difficult part of this whole dish is sourcing woodcock. Even with a network of amazing suppliers, they still remain elusive.

The woodcock should be plucked and gutted. Clean the head and beak with a scouring pad as they are served as part of the dish and should be as clean as possible.

All basic garnishes and the sauce should be prepared in advance. The woodcock requires less than 10 minutes' cooking from start to finish.

Sauté the woodcock (including its head) in butter, turning frequently – this should take 3–4 minutes. Rest for 5 minutes. At the same time pan fry the foie gras; deglaze the pan with xeres vinegar and season. The woodcock, which require very little cooking, should be served 'pink'.

To finish, make sure that all the garnish is hot. Remove the breasts from the bird, place the foie gras between the breasts and skewer with the beak. Split the head open with a sharp cook's knife.

Al's advice
Please try eating the brains. Every single guest who ate woodcock in the restaurant last game season ate the brains!!!!!

Guinea Fowl

Breast of guinea fowl, ballotine of leg, wild garlic & morille ravioli, white truffle cream sauce

Guinea fowl, also known as the African pheasant, is a very lean bird, rich in protein yet containing only half the fat of chicken. Wild garlic is renowned for its anti-fungal and immune-boosting properties and for supporting the blood system and heart.

Serves 4

Guinea Fowl

1 free-range guinea fowl, approx. 1.8kg

75g unsalted butter

75ml olive oil

Leg Ballotine

smoked bacon, garlic

egg, parsley

Ravioli of Wild Garlic

200g chicken mousse

(see basics 87)

100g cooked morilles

25g butter

wild garlic leaves

White Truffle Cream Sauce

(see basics 41)

Garnish

100g fresh morilles

50g unsalted butter

12 blanched asparagus spears

Preparation

Prepare the guinea fowl by first removing the legs. Take the bird down to a crown and remove the wishbone. Reserve the crown in the refrigerator.

Bone out the guinea fowl legs, ensuring that you remove all sinews and bone. Trim off any excess fat.

Make the stuffing for the legs by mincing the guinea fowl trim and bacon. Finely chop the garlic and stir into the minced meat with the egg and parsley. This should require no seasoning as the smoked bacon is usually salty enough.

Lay the boned legs skin side down and fill with the farce to form a sausage shape. Wrap the leg around the farce and roll tightly in cling film. Poach at 65°C for 30 minutes and refresh.

To make the ravioli, prepare the chicken mousse following the basic recipe. Sauté the morilles in the butter, season and allow to cool. When cold, chop roughly and stir into the chicken mousse. Lay out the wild garlic leaves. Place 1 tablespoon of the mousse mixture onto a garlic leaf and spread evenly. Cover with another garlic leaf, ensuring that no mousse is showing.

To cook the guinea fowl, sauté the crown skin side down in the butter and oil until golden brown all over. Place in the oven for 25 minutes. Baste, add the guinea fowl leg ballotines and cook for a further 25 minutes. Allow to rest for 15 minutes before serving. Unlike chicken, guinea fowl can be served a little pink.

To cook the wild garlic ravioli, steam gently for 2–3 minutes until the mousse is cooked.

Al's advice
If you would prefer not to bone the legs, confit guinea fowl legs can be used as a welcome alternative to duck

John Dory

Pan-fried John Dory, cassoulet of haricots blancs, smoked ham rillette, pea & ham velouté

John Dory is a rich source of protein and omega-3 essential fats which are vital nutrients – essential for the body but that cannot be made by the body. These essential fats are great cholesterol busters, mood enhancers and excellent 'brain food'.

Serves 4

John Dory

4 x 100g pieces John Dory
fillet
50ml olive oil
50g unsalted butter
lemon juice

Ham Rillette

500g smoked ham hock
white chicken stock
(see basics 1)
bay leaf, celery, onion
1 tbs Dijon mustard
75g foie gras fat
olive oil

Cassoulet

150g haricots blancs
750ml ham stock
(see basics 104)
thyme, bay leaf
100g fresh peas, blanched

Pea Velouté

500ml ham stock
300g frozen peas
white truffle oil
salt and white pepper

Garnish

picked pea shoots
smoked bacon powder
(see basics 15)
white truffle oil

Preparation

This is actually quite a simple dish if you prepare the basics in the right order.

Cook the smoked ham hock 24 hours in advance. Bring the chicken stock to the boil, add the ham, thyme, bay leaf, celery and onion, and simmer for 2 hours or until the ham is tender and almost falling off the bone. Remove the ham from the pan carefully and allow to cool. When still warm, flake the meat off the bone, discarding any excess fat. Place in a large bowl and add the Dijon mustard and the foie gras fat. (You could use duck fat as a substitute.) Form the meat into a large sausage and wrap tightly in cling film. Put in the refrigerator for a minimum of 12 hours. Strain the stock through a fine sieve and store in the refrigerator overnight.

Soak the haricot beans overnight in cold water. Drain and cook in 750ml of the ham stock with the herbs. Simmer for 90 minutes or until the beans are soft, then strain off the stock and reserve. Take 75g of the cooked beans and blend to a sauce consistency with 100ml of the stock. Mix back into the beans and add the blanched peas. Set aside.

For the velouté, heat 500ml of stock until boiling. Pour directly onto the frozen peas, and blend until smooth. Pass through a fine sieve, reserving the pulp for garnishing the rillette. Season the velouté with truffle oil, salt and white pepper.

To finish the dish, cut the rillette into eight discs and sauté in a little olive oil.

Warm the cassoulet gently. Heat the pea velouté at the last minute or it will lose its freshness.

To cook the John Dory, heat a non-stick pan until hot. Add the olive oil and quickly colour the fish on one side – about 1 minute – then turn the fish and add the butter. Season and baste, then cook for a further 90 seconds, basting the fish as you go. Add a dash of lemon juice and rest for 2 minutes.

Al's advice
Pea velouté made with frozen peas sounds like a real 'cowboy' way of cooking. I have yet to find a better or more flavoursome way.

Lamb Rump

Moroccan lamb, harissa-spiced couscous, confit cherry tomatoes & roasting juices

Moroccan flavours in abundance, influenced by Will (from Bristol).

Serves 4

Lamb Rump

2 x 240g lamb rumps

Moroccan lamb marinade

(see basics 201)

75ml olive oil

Lamb Jus

(see basics 32)

Chickpea Salsa

(see basics 103)

Harissa-Spiced Couscous

harissa (see basics 100)

couscous (see basics 101)

Garnish

moutabal

(see basics 102)

dried coriander

(see basics 69)

28 pieces confit tomato

(see basics 45)

Preparation

Marinate the lamb in the refrigerator for a minimum of 48 hours before you want to serve it. In an ideal world, you would do this for four days!

Lamb jus can be made at least 24 hours in advance.

Make the moutabal and chickpea salsa on the day you want to serve the dish.

This dish is served ambient – the lamb will be hot, but the garnish should be at room temperature. Remove the couscous and salsa from the refrigerator 30 minutes in advance of serving.

To cook the lamb, first scrape off any excess marinade. Caramelise the lamb evenly in olive oil in a non-stick pan, ensuring that it does not catch and burn – this will take 4–5 minutes. Then put the lamb in the oven at 190°C for 8–9 minutes, or until the lamb is medium rare, turning twice. (Lamb is not a meat that eats well when cooked rare.) Rest for a further 10 minutes.

Al's advice
You could use almost any cut of lamb for this dish. Fillet, loin, shoulder or leg could all be rubbed with the marinade and cooked accordingly.

Turbot

Tronchon of turbot, spring vegetables, new season morilles, morille cream sauce

A 'tronchon' is cut from a large flat fish by splitting it in two down the length of the spine, then cutting the two halves into portions. With a round fish like a salmon it would be referred to as a 'darne'. This technique is one of the best ways of cooking a thick and meaty fish like a large turbot. By cooking it on the bone you reduce shrinkage, increase flavour and add to presentation.

Serves 8

Turbot

1 x 3.5–4kg turbot

olive oil

butter

lemon juice

Morille Cream Sauce

(see basics 10)

Garnish

400g fresh morilles

40 asparagus spears

200g fresh peas

200g fresh broad beans

400g spring cabbage

split haricots verts

split haricots jaunes

trompette de la morte

cèpe powder

(see basics 57)

Preparation

As with a lot of the dishes in this book, the quality and freshness of the produce involved is the secret to its success. Large turbot are quite difficult to find and very expensive.

I have specified this recipe for eight guests as you require a large turbot to achieve the perfect 'tronchon'.

To cut a tronchon of turbot, place the fish dark side up on a chopping board. Remove the fins and side skirt with scissors, and cut the head off using a serrated knife. To split the fish, cut it lengthways following the spine; the easiest way to do this is to use a serrated knife. When you have cut the fish into two, trim both ends then cut the fish into four large, even slices. Remove any of the blood line that remains.

Morille cream sauce should be made on the day. Basic vegetable preparation should also all be done on the day.

To cook the turbot, gently heat a non-stick pan. Start the turbot over a medium heat in the olive oil and cook until lightly coloured. Add the butter and take to beurre noisette stage. Turn the fish over and colour on the other side in the foaming butter. It is important to baste the fish during the cooking process, after 3–4 minutes on each side; season well and add a dash of lemon juice. Allow to rest for 5 minutes before serving.

Al's advice
Large brill or plaice could be used instead of turbot.

Squab

Roast squab & black truffle, choucroute with Morteau sausage, roasted cèpes & salsify, truffle & Madeira jus

A luxury dish to prepare – the finest Anjou squab larded with Perigord truffle. Truffle and squab pigeon are a natural marriage.

Serves 4

Squab Pigeon

4 x 500g Anjou squab

pigeons

100g fresh Perigord truffles

olive oil

butter

Pigeon Leg Confit

8 pigeon legs

sea salt and crushed black

peppercorns

thyme

100g duck fat

Perigord Truffle &

Madeira Jus

(see basics 97)

Garnish

thyme and juniper gnocchi

(see basics 99)

JBR's choucroute

(see basics 98)

24 slices Morteau sausage

truffle oil

haricots verts

trompette de la morte

Preparation

Prepare the pigeons by gutting them and removing the heads. Take the squabs down to a crown, and keep all the bones, including the neck, for the sauce.

Remove the legs for the confit. Sprinkle with sea salt, pepper and thyme and allow to marinate for 2 hours. With the oven at 120°C, cook the legs in the duck fat for 90 minutes, until tender.

Take out the wishbone from each squab. Gently peel back the skin from the neck end of the breast to halfway down the breast. Place 25g sliced raw truffle onto each breast and cover with the skin. Set aside in the refrigerator.

Make the truffle and Madeira jus, following the basic recipe and using the pigeon bones.

The gnocchi and choucroute can be prepared in advance.

To cook and serve, colour the pigeon crowns skin side down in the olive oil over a medium heat. Turn onto their backs and add the butter. Take to beurre noisette and baste the crowns with the butter. Add the confit pigeon legs to the pan then place in the oven at 190°C for 4 minutes, basting every minute. Remove from the pan and rest for 5 minutes.

Sauté the gnocchi in butter to give a little colour. Reheat the choucroute and warm the sauce.

Season the pigeon breasts, and serve immediately.

Al's advice

Squab pigeon is not to be confused with its wild relation, the wood pigeon. Squabs have much lighter flesh and a milder flavour.

Pyrenean Lamb

Tasting plate of milk-fed lamb, braised shank & shoulder, roast best end, confit neck, pan-fried kidney & sweetbreads, basil pomme purée, Niçoise garnish

A true test of any chef's craft with a whole animal, encompassing skills such as roasting, braising, confiting and pan-frying, and the virtue of patience.

Serves 4

Confit Neck
200g lamb neck
25g rock salt
25g crushed black peppercorns
2 sprigs rosemary, roughly chopped
500g lamb fat

Shoulder & Shanks
600g boned and rolled lamb shoulder
4 x 120g baby lamb shanks
150g unsalted butter
100ml olive oil
1 litre white chicken stock (see basics 1)
1 litre lamb stock (see basics 226)
bunch of rosemary
2 heads garlic

Roast Best End
400g French-trimmed best end
50ml olive oil

Sweetbreads
160g lamb's sweetbreads, blanched and peeled
75g unsalted butter

Kidney
150g lamb's kidney
olive oil

Garnish
basil pomme purée (see basics 188)
fennel purée (see basics 227)
tomato pistou (see basics 183)
braised fennel (see basics 14)
confit baby aubergine (see basics 193)
confit tomato (see basics 45)
confit garlic (see basics 194)
split haricot verts
dried basil leaves
extra virgin olive oil

Preparation

Start by doing all the basic butchery and making the lamb stock.

Lamb neck, shoulder and shanks can all be cooked at least a day in advance.

All garnishes can be prepared a day in advance.

Marinate the lamb neck in the salt, pepper and rosemary for 12 hours. Place in a casserole dish and cover with the lamb fat. Simmer very gently on the stove for 2 hours, then remove from the fat and allow to cool. Reserve the fat to reuse.

Caramelise the lamb shanks and shoulder in foaming butter and olive oil until golden brown. Pour off the excess fat. Place the meat in a large casserole dish and cover with the chicken and lamb stocks, rosemary and garlic. Bring to the boil and skim. Put in a medium oven at 150°C for 2–3 hours until the meat is tender, then remove the shoulder and shanks from the stock and allow to cool. While the shoulder is still warm, roll in cling film to form a large cylinder. When cold, cut into large discs and place in the refrigerator with the shanks. Strain the stock through a fine sieve and reduce to a sauce consistency.

To cook and finish the lamb, caramelise the best end of lamb in the olive oil, skin side down, in a non-stick pan over a medium heat. Cook until the fat is rendered down and the skin is dark brown, then turn over and colour for 2–3 minutes. Turn the lamb back onto the skin and place in the oven at 190°C for 7–8 minutes. Allow to rest for 10 minutes.

While the lamb rack is in the oven, place the shoulder, neck and shanks in the oven to reheat for about 15 minutes. The shoulder and neck should require no liquid but the shank should have a little of the lamb stock poured over; use this to baste the meat.

At the last minute, reheat the garnish and cook the sweetbreads in the foaming butter until golden brown. Sauté the kidney in olive oil for 2 minutes. Season all the meat and serve.

Sea Bass

Fillet of sea bass, braised fennel, confit artichoke,
fennel purée, pan-fried scallops, liquorice & red wine jus

Serves 4

Sea Bass

4 x 120g paves sea bass
fillet from 2.5–3kg sea bass
50ml olive oil
50g unsalted butter
lemon juice

Braised Fennel

2 large heads fennel
50ml olive oil
500ml vegetable nage
(see basics 11)
1 sprig thyme
25g fennel seeds
2 star anise
bay leaf

Fennel Purée

(see basics 227)

Confit Tomato

(see basics 45)

Confit Artichoke

(see basics 233)

Liquorice Sauce

(see basics 230)

Garnish

12 hand-dived scallops
50g fennel cress

Preparation

Prepare the braised fennel by taking a large bulb and cutting two large slices through the centre, keeping the root attached. The fennel should look like a flame. Keep all the trim for the fennel purée. In a casserole dish, heat the olive oil and evenly colour the fennel flames on both sides. Cover with the vegetable nage. Add the thyme, fennel seeds, star anise and bay leaf. Bring to the boil and simmer for 20–25 minutes, until the fennel is tender, then allow to cool in the liquor. When cold, remove from the cooking liquor and set aside.

Use the fennel trimmings to make the fennel purée, following the basic recipe.

All other basics can be prepared 24 hours in advance.

To finish the dish, colour the cooked fennel in a little olive oil. Place the tomatoes and artichokes under a medium grill until warm, but not too hot, and warm the fennel purée and liquorice sauce.

To cook the bass, warm a non-stick pan over a medium heat. Start the sea bass skin side down and gradually increase the heat. When the skin in nice and coloured, add the butter and turn. Baste with the butter and continue to cook over a medium heat, ensuring that the butter does not get too hot. The fish requires 2–3 minutes on each side. Season well and add lemon juice, then rest the fish for 3 minutes. While you are waiting, cook the scallops following a similar method but allowing 1 minute each side.

Al's advice
This is a perfect dinner party dish as all the basic work can be done a day in advance and the sea bass and scallops are cooked at the last minute.

Suckling Pig

Tasting plate of suckling pig, sage gnocchi, smoked apple purée & roasting jus

Suckling pig is best when still very young – under 50 days old. The meat will be very tender and delicate. The whole animal is served, displaying about every basic cooking technique known: from tempura of crispy ears, poached and roasted stuffed saddle, roasted best end, braised shoulder, poached choux farcie and confit belly to the smallest of glazed pig's trotters.

Serves 4

Braising Liquor

1kg suckling pig bones, chopped

100ml olive oil

2 large onions

2 heads garlic

2 sprigs thyme

750ml white wine

1.5 litres brown chicken stock (see basics 2)

1.5 litres white chicken stock (see basics 1)

Trotter (Pied de Cochon)

4 baby pig's trotters

50g smoked bacon, minced

50g shoulder meat, minced

500ml braising liquor

Braised Shoulder

400g boned and rolled shoulder

100ml olive oil

700ml braising liquor

Stuffed Saddle

1 suckling pig saddle

1 onion, finely diced

50ml olive oil

50g fresh breadcrumbs

16 large sage leaves

2 suckling pig fillets

6 thin slices smoked bacon

500ml white chicken stock (see basics 1)

Preparation

All the butchery work to start the day! I have broken each part down into individual servings as I doubt you would ever be able to do this whole dish!!!

Chop all the bones, place in a large roasting tray with the olive oil, and roast in the oven at 200°C. When caramelised, add the onions, garlic and thyme and cook for a further 10 minutes.

Pour the bones into a colander to remove the excess fat. Place in a large saucepan. Add the white wine and reduce by half. Add the stocks, bring to the boil, skim and simmer for 2 hours. Pass through a sieve and reserve.

Bone out the trotters, ensuring that the skin is kept intact as much as possible. Place in the braising liquor and simmer for 2 hours until tender. Remove from the liquor and allow to cool. When cold, mix the smoked bacon and shoulder meat together and stuff into the trotters. Roll tightly in cling film. When ready to serve, prick the cling film with a pin and simmer the trotters in the cooking liquor for 15 minutes. Glaze under a hot grill for 2–3 minutes, basting with a little of the jus.

Colour the shoulder in the olive oil until golden brown. Place in a casserole dish and cover with the braising liquor. Bring to the boil, skim and place in the oven at 150°C for 2–3 hours until tender. Remove from the liquor and allow to cool. When cool, roll tightly in cling film and allow to set. When set, slice and reheat in the oven at 190°C for 10 minutes with a little of the liquor.

Bone the whole saddle, ensuring that the skin that runs along the backbone is kept intact. Sauté the onion in the olive oil for 5 minutes without colouring. Add the breadcrumbs and a chopped sage leaf, season and allow to cool. Line the inside of the saddle evenly with the sage leaves. Lay the fillets down the middle of the saddle then spoon on the onion mixture. Fold over the sage leaves to form a long sausage. Roll the saddle around the sage sausage, wrap in the finely sliced bacon and tie with fine string. Poach in the chicken stock for 10 minutes. Remove and dry thoroughly. Roast in a hot oven for 10 minutes. Rest for 15 minutes, slice and serve.

Confit Belly

200g suckling pig belly
100g rock salt
50g crushed black pepper
2 sprigs rosemary
500g duck fat

Choux Farcie

4 blanched cabbage leaves
75g pork shoulder, minced
75g smoked bacon, minced
2 cloves garlic, finely chopped
3 sage leaves, chopped
braising liquor to cover

Crispy Ear

1 suckling pig ear
350ml braising liquor
flour, egg, breadcrumbs

Best End

180g French-trimmed suckling pig best end
50ml olive oil
50g unsalted butter

Garnish

20 pieces sage gnocchi (see basics 182)
100g black pudding
75g broad beans
75g fresh peas
20 pieces roast baby onions
120g shredded cabbage
vegetable emulsion (see basics 59)
4 sage leaves
50g unsalted butter
20 apple balls, cooked in 100g caster sugar until caramelised

Marinate the pork belly in the salt, pepper and rosemary for 36 hours. Scrape off any excess salt mixture. Place in the duck fat and cook in the oven at 130°C for 4–5 hours. When cooked, remove carefully from the fat and press under a medium weight in the refrigerator. To serve, cut into pavés and place in a non-stick pan, skin side down, in the oven at 190°C for 10–15 minutes.

For the choux farcie, lay the blanched cabbage leaves on a tea towel and dry thoroughly. Mix all the ingredients together and spread evenly onto the cabbage leaves. Roll the cabbage into a long thin sausage shape, trim off the ends and roll tightly in muslin cloth. Cover with the braising liquor and simmer for 10–15 minutes. Remove the muslin and serve.

Very carefully blowtorch the pig's ear to remove any hairs! Run under cold running water for 1 hour and dry thoroughly. Place in the braising liquor and simmer for 6–8 hours until soft and tender. Remove from the liquor and allow to cool overnight in the refrigerator. To serve, cut into long strips and dip in the flour, egg and breadcrumbs (pané). Deep fry at 190°C for 2–3 minutes.

Cooking the best end is the simplest of tasks. Heat the oil in a non-stick pan and add the best end skin side down. When the skin is golden brown and crispy, turn over and colour the other side of the meat. Turn back onto the skin and put in the oven at 190°C for 4–5 minutes. Remove from the oven and allow to rest for 10 minutes.

Al's advice
This is one of the hardest and most challenging dishes to serve. For this reason I suggest maybe doing only two of the cuts at any one time.

'The very foundation of life relies on food; creating beautiful harmonies from nature's larder is one of the greatest gifts mankind possesses. Food is about bringing people together, it is about comfort and it is about memories. Nothing is more powerful. Food glorious food.'

Chef John Campbell

'Food is much more than something that is needed for sustenance; it should be a great pleasure.
It is not necessary to use extravagant or expensive ingredients as the simplest produce such as potatoes, leeks or eggs prepared with care and love will make family and friends happy.'

Chef Michel Roux

cheese3

'Food and wine matching plays an integral role in the whole "dining" experience. Whenever we are looking at working with a new producer I taste the wines without food alongside Stephen, my Sommelier, and find the right wines that will work with our style of food. It is much easier to adapt a dish to complement the wine than the other way. You can change a wine's characteristics by 10–20% by choosing the correct glass and temperature; however, it is relatively simple to increase or decrease acidity, sweetness or richness in a dish.'

Chef Alan Murchison

Roquefort

Probably the best blue cheese in the world. The blue penicillin added to most blue cheeses is actually named *Penicillium roqueforti* after the great Roquefort cheese. Roquefort is produced from ewe's milk. The cheese is matured in caves under the town of Roquefort-sur-Soulzon, which is situated on the southern coast of France. This maturation process allows the cheese to be moist, pungent and salty.

Accompaniment Pairing
Fig & Mustard Chutney
(see basics 107)

Figs are already a classic match to Roquefort, fruity yet savoury to counter the salty, slightly bitter, acidic flavour of the cheese.

Wine Pairing
Sauternes or Monbazillac
(Classic Match for Roquefort)

Blissful

Produced by Ian Arnett in Exmoor, this cheese is unusual in that it is produced using buffalo's milk. The buffalo herd is not native to England. As you may have guessed, they were bought in from the southern USA. The blue in the cheese is not as pronounced as in Roquefort, reducing the acidity and resulting in a lighter, creamier blue. Buffalo's milk is almost white in appearance, and has a slightly sweet tangy character to it – flavours that marry into a blue cheese beautifully.

Accompaniment Pairing
Muscat Grapes

Wine Pairing
Chenin Blanc (sweet)

Valencay

Produced in the Normandy region of France, made with raw goat's milk. The cheese carries a soft, creamy, full goat's cheese flavour, which is well enhanced by the ash coating. The cheese is shaped as a flat-topped pyramid. There are many theories as to the reason for this but the most popular is that when Napoleon returned from his unsuccessful escapades in Egypt he went to Paris to have dinner with Prince Talleyrand. As he was telling the prince of his battles, a cheese came to table in the shape of a pyramid. This angered Napoleon greatly so he jumped to his feet, drew his sword and chopped the top off the cheese. It has been produced in this shape ever since.

Accompaniment Pairing
White Truffle Honey
(see basics 48)

Wine Pairing
Sancerre or Muscadet

Broccio Passu

Simply known as Broccio, this cheese is produced from ewe's milk on the island of Corsica. A Corsican speciality, it is made almost entirely from lacto serum and then coated in ash, which gives the cheese a very bitter, maybe even slightly spicy flavour. It is said that the Corsicans like to eat a small piece of this cheese instead of coffee with breakfast, as the bitter flavours can be similar. The leaf on the top is a mystery – presumably an ancient Corsican tradition.

Accompaniment Pairing
Celery

Wine Pairing
Viognier

Langres

This cheese is produced in the village of Langres high up in the hills of Champagne. It is made from cow's milk and then coated in brine, which gives it that amazing orange colour. The cheese is small and round but has a well or dip in the top. On its own the cheese has quite a dry, smoky bacon flavour that is medium strong. However, the people of Champagne like to pour champagne into the well before slicing the cheese open and devouring it.

Accompaniment Pairing
Quince Jelly (see basics 108)

Wine Pairing
Pommery Springtime

Morbier

Morbier is a cheese made from cow's milk in the Jura region of France. It is a semi-hard cheese, with a slightly rubbery texture. Its most interesting feature is the line of ash running down the centre of the cheese. This separates the morning milking from the evening milking. It was first produced in this way by a farmer who wished to keep a little cheese over for his family. He coated this cheese in ash to preserve it one evening. In the morning he had some more cheese left over but instead of taking the ash away he simply piled the new cheese on top. In the end the flavour wasn't too bad and Morbier was formed. The cheese holds a light, delicate, fruity, nutty flavour.

Accompaniment Pairing
Piccalilli (see basics 109)

Wine Pairing
Juraçon Sec

Bosworth Ash

Bosworth Ash is a traditional English goat's cheese log from Tamworth in Staffordshire produced as a thin, round log with a penicillin rind that has a thin layer of ash inside. A young Bosworth is firm and breakable with a fudge-like texture, and is sweet and nutty without an overpowering goat flavour. The matured Bosworth is slightly stronger in flavour; the sweetness is lost but the nutty flavour is much more pronounced and the cheese is altogether richer and fuller.

Accompaniment Pairing
Walnut & Raisin Bread
(see basics 110)

Wine Pairing
Amontillado Sherry or
dry Madeira

Wigmore

An English Brie-style cheese produced by Anne and Andy Wigmore in Riseley, Berkshire. Gold medal at the British Cheese Awards three times. A light ewe's milk cheese that is in no way overpowering, it is delicate and floral, cool and refreshing. Vegetarian.

Accompaniment Pairing
Apple & Rosemary Jam
(see basics 111)

Wine Pairing
lightly sweet white,
e.g. Muscat de Rivesaltes

St Simeon

A French cow's milk Brie from the town of
St Simeon in France. Served in a plastic shell
to protect the soft delicate rind. The rind is
slightly orange in colour yet entirely edible.
The cheese is triple crème and when ripe is soft
and creamy enough to serve with a spoon.

Accompaniment Pairing
Caraway Seed Biscuit
(see basics 113)

Wine Pairing
Arbois Vin Jaune

Epoisses

A cow's milk cheese made in the Burgundy
region of France that has been washed in brine
and marc de Bourgogne. Marc is made during
the production of Burgundy, from the pips and
skins of the wine grapes. The marc gives the
cheese a very pungent yet distinctive flavour,
which is spicy and meaty. It has a very soft and
creamy texture.

Accompaniment Pairing
Confit Red Onion
(see basics 112)

Wine Pairing
White fine Burgundy or
late harvest Gewürztraminer

Stinking Bishop

Cow's milk cheese made by Charles Martell in Gloucestershire. The name, although apt, does not in fact refer to the aromatic qualities of the cheese. The rind of the cheese is washed in perry. The variety of pear used to make this perry was called … Stinking Bishop! Stinking Bishop was of course bought to fame by the Wallace and Gromit movie; however, Charles shuns the spotlight, and refuses to increase production to match demand. The reason behind this is that when the cheese was first made the intention was to raise awareness of the quality of milk produced by the Gloucestershire cow; Charles is a member of the preservation society.

The cheese is as pungent as the name suggests but not quite as powerful. It is spongy in texture, with a medium-strong farmhouse flavour, which is complemented perfectly by the perry-washed rind

Accompaniment Pairing
Radishes

Wine Pairing
Pale Ale or a very light red Burgundy

Montgomery Cheddar

The king of English Cheddars! A list of honours longer than your arm. Available at different ages, smoked or unsmoked. The younger ten-month cheddar is more delicate, with more citrus notes; it is still slightly moist, whereas the more mature–aged up to two years – is more crumbly in texture and powerful in flavour

Accompaniment Pairing
Celery Salt Biscuit
(see basics 114)

Wine Pairing
Cider (dry)

desserts

Iced Nougat Parfait

Iced nougat parfait, amaretto ice cream,
Frangelico jelly

Serves 4

Iced Parfait

25g caster sugar

50g honey

10g glucose

60g egg whites

50g crushed praline

40g confit orange zest,
finely chopped

25g nibbed almonds

25g green pistachio nuts,
roughly chopped

250g lightly whipped cream

Amaretto Ice Cream

250g milk

150g whipping cream

60g egg yolks

45g caster sugar

20g almond paste

10g almond milk

20g amaretto

Chocolate Crêpe

(see basics 135)

Frangelico Jelly

(see basics 134)

To finish

pulled caramel hazelnuts

crushed praline

Preparation

Start the basic preparation 24 hours in advance. Make the parfait by cooking the sugar, honey and glucose to 121°C. Whip the egg whites to ribbon stage and slowly pour on the sugar; keep whipping until cold. When cold, fold in the praline, orange zest and nuts, then gently fold in the cream until smooth. Pipe into 6cm diameter × 4cm high moulds and freeze at −21°C.

To make the ice cream, boil the milk and the cream, then whisk in the egg yolks and sugar and cook out as you would a basic anglaise. Remove from the heat and whisk in the almond paste, almond milk and amaretto. Pass through a fine sieve and cool down over ice. Freeze to −21°C and then Pacojet or churn as normal in an ice cream machine.

Basic recipes for the chocolate crêpe and Frangelico jelly can be made 4–6 hours in advance.

To finish the dish, remove the parfait from the freezer 10 minutes before serving and roll it in the crushed praline.

Al's advice
The pulled hazelnuts are really simple to do. Make a dark caramel, skewer the hazelnuts with cocktail sticks and dip into the caramel. Hang them upside down until the caramel sets. Remove the cocktail sticks and serve.

Blood Orange

Carpaccio of blood orange, hazelnut financier & lemon sorbet

A technique shown to me by my crazy Dutch friend Marcin Beaufort. Very light and fresh, it also works well with pink grapefruit.

Serves 4

Blood Orange Carpaccio

2 leaves gelatine

250g blood orange juice

50g Campari

500g blood orange

segments

Orange Tuile

85g butter

170g caster sugar

zest of 1 orange

85g plain flour

85g orange juice

Hazelnut Financier

(see basics 152)

Lemon Sorbet

(see basics 214)

To finish

orange confit

(see basics 131)

picked mint

dried orange slices

(see basics 55)

Preparation

Prepare the carpaccio at least 24 hours in advance. Soak the gelatine in cold water for 15 minutes and strain well. Warm the blood orange juice, then add the soaked gelatine and dissolve. Add the Campari and pour over the blood orange segments. Set aside and allow to cool. When it is starting to set, you must work quickly.

On a clean work surface, lay out a double layer of cling film, 60cm × 35cm. Place the setting orange mixture onto the centre of the cling film, and carefully roll the cling film over the mixture to encase it. Form into a large 'sausage' shape, squeezing out any excess air, and roll tightly. Tie up each end and place in the freezer at –18°C for 24 hours.

To make the orange tuile, melt the butter and leave to cool. Mix together the sugar, zest and flour. Incorporate the orange juice, then fold in the melted butter. Spread thinly and evenly on a non-stick tray and cook at 180°C for approx. 6 minutes, until golden brown. Allow to cool.

Hazelnut financier and lemon sorbet can be made 24 hours in advance, following the basic recipes.

When ready to serve the carpaccio, remove the cling film and cut into 2mm thick slices. Serve immediately.

Al's advice
The blood orange carpaccio
can also be sliced and plated in
advance and then put back into
the freezer until you are ready to serve.

Chocolate Fondant

Warm chocolate fondant, banana cake & Galliano ice cream

Cocoa beans are very rich in antioxidants, especially flavonoids which help to absorb damaging free radicals. There is much evidence to suggest that chocolate is an aphrodisiac and mood enhancer due to the fact that it raises serotonin levels and releases endorphins.

Serves 4

Warm Chocolate Fondant

115g 70% bitter chocolate
112g unsalted butter
60g plain flour, sieved
100g egg whites
85g caster sugar

Caramel Mousse

97g caster sugar
55g double cream, warmed
2 leaves gelatine
45g egg yolks
250g double cream, lightly whipped

Banana & Galliano Ice Cream

250g plain vanilla ice cream base (see basics 175)
250g banana purée
30g crème de banane
20g lime juice

Banana Cake

(see basics 160)

Brandy Snap

(see basics 161)

Honeycomb

(see basics 158)

To finish

caramel sauce
(see basics 157)
100g diced banana
and lime juice

Preparation

The fondants are relatively easy. Melt the chocolate and butter in a bain-marie, then whisk in the flour, making sure the mixture is smooth. Make a meringue using the egg whites and sugar, being careful not to overwhip the whites. Gently fold the meringue into the chocolate mixture. Pour into well-greased rings and place in the refrigerator until required.

To make the caramel mousse, put 62g caster sugar in a pan and make a dark caramel. Remove from the heat and slowly add the cream – be very careful! Return to a gentle heat and warm until the caramel and cream are completely smooth, then allow to cool. Soak the gelatine in cold water for 15 minutes and strain well. Make an anglaise using the yolks, the remaining sugar and the caramel liquid. Add the gelatine, whisk well and strain through a fine sieve. Cool over ice until the mixture thickens, then fold in the whipped cream.

Banana ice cream is simple. Combine all the ingredients together and blend in a Thermomix or food blender for 3 minutes. Pass through a fine sieve into a Pacojet container, freeze to –21°C for 12 hours and blitz as normal, or churn in a conventional ice cream machine and use as required.

All other basics can be made on the day you wish to serve them.

To cook the fondants, place in a pre-heated oven at 175°C for 8 minutes. Remove from the oven and allow to rest for 1 minute. Unmould and serve.

Al's advice
There are a lot of components to this 'restaurant dish'. Just the fondant and caramel mousse can be stunning for a simple dessert.

Peach

Poached peach with vanilla mousse, raspberry jelly & champagne granite

'Peach Melba'. Peach, raspberry and vanilla heaven!

Serves 4

Poached Peach

4 large ripe yellow peaches
750g water
450g caster sugar
juice of 1 lemon

Vanilla Mousse

2g leaf gelatine
20g whipping cream
70g vanilla anglaise
(see basics 179)
1 vanilla pod, seeds only
125g lightly whipped cream

Champagne Granite

100ml peach cooking liquor
10g sugar
75ml rose champagne

Peach & Raspberry Purées

100g white peach purée
(see basics 165)
100g pink peach purée
100g raspberry purée
(see basics 166)
sugar and lemon juice, to
taste

Raspberry & Elderflower Jelly
(see basics 215)

Plain Tuile
(see basics 126)

To finish
dried raspberry powder
12 fresh raspberries

Preparation

The peaches can be cooked 24 hours in advance. Place the water, sugar and lemon juice in a medium pan and bring to a light boil. Add the peaches and poach gently until tender. Cool and place in the refrigerator.

For the vanilla mousse, soak the gelatine in cold water for 15 minutes, then strain well. Gently warm the 20g whipping cream, add the vanilla seeds and dissolve the gelatine. Pour onto the vanilla anglaise and whisk well. Gently fold in the whipped cream and set aside.

For the granite, simmer the peach liquor and add the sugar. Allow to cool, then mix in the champagne and place in the freezer overnight. When frozen, scrape with a fork until it resembles snow, and reserve in the freezer.

For the peach purées and raspberry purées, add sugar and lemon juice to taste and reduce to the correct consistency – it is difficult to give exact measurements as the acidity in the fruit can vary greatly.

The raspberry and elderflower jelly and the tuile can be prepared on the day.

To finish the dish, remove the skin and the stone from the poached peaches; try to keep the peaches in one piece. Pipe the vanilla mousse into the cavity vacated by the stone. Arrange raspberry jelly and purées around the plate, add the granite and serve.

Al's advice
A very simple and effective dessert. Ensure that the raspberries and peaches are of the highest quality.

Lychee

Lychee bavarois, passion fruit jelly, coconut sorbet, exotic fruit salsa

The great thing about exotic fruits is that they are almost always in season somewhere. Enjoy this dessert with a superb Göttelmann Riesling Auslese, available from Iris Ellman at the Wine Barn.

Serves 4

Lychee Bavarois

185g caster sugar

100g water

4 leaves gelatine

250g lychee purée

250g lightly whipped cream

Passion Fruit Jelly

30g stock syrup

(basics 178)

1 leaf gelatine

50g orange juice

45g passion fruit juice

passion fruit seeds

Coconut Sorbet

400g coconut purée

40g caster sugar

40g unsweetened natural

yoghurt

10ml lime juice

Exotic Fruit Salsa

guava, mango, pineapple

– all cut into small,

uniform dice

To finish

dried star fruit

Preparation

Start the lychee bavarois 24 hours in advance. Make a light stock syrup using the sugar and water. Soak the gelatine in cold water for 15 minutes, strain well and add to the syrup. Whisk in the lychee purée and cool over ice until thick. Fold in the cream and set in rectanglular moulds – don't fill right to the top of the moulds as you will need to add a layer of jelly. When set, place in the refrigerator.

For the passion fruit jelly, bring the syrup to the boil, dissolve the gelatine and whisk in the juices. Chill over ice until beginning to set. Sprinkle the set lychee bavarois with passion fruit seeds then cover the tops of the bavarois thinly and evenly with the jelly. Leave to set in the refrigerator – allow 3–4 hours.

Make the sorbet base the day before serving. Boil 100g of the coconut purée, then add the sugar and dissolve. Mix into the rest of the purée. Whisk in the yoghurt and lime juice, then churn in an ice cream machine or freeze to −21°C and Pacojet as normal.

Al's advice

Lychee purée can be replaced with mango, coconut or guava

135

Strawberry

Wild strawberry marshmallow, iced vanilla parfait & spiced strawberry purée

When possible try to use the fragrant Mara des Bois strawberry from Kent. The season is very short but the taste and texture are truly unique.

Serves 4

Vanilla Parfait

(see basics 174)

Spiced Strawberry Sauce

(see basics 176)

Marshmallow

80g egg whites

190g caster sugar

50ml water

3 leaves gelatine

seeds of 1 large vanilla pod

Wild Strawberry Sorbet

250g wild strawberry purée

dash of lemon juice

60g sugar syrup

(see basics 180)

To finish

fresh strawberries

crushed pink peppercorns

vanilla anglaise

(see basics 179)

Preparation

Make the vanilla parfait and spiced strawberry sauce, following the basic recipes. The parfait can be kept in the freezer for a week easily.

To make the marshmallow, place the egg whites in an electric mixing bowl. At this point put the sugar and water in a pan and heat to 115°C. Soak the gelatine in cold water for 15 minutes, strain well and set aside. Start whisking the whites on full speed, and when the sugar reaches 121°C pour it carefully down the side of the bowl onto the whisked whites. Ensure that the syrup does not hit the whisk. Now add the soaked gelatine and scrape in the vanilla seeds. Continue whisking at a medium speed until cool. Fill 6cm dome moulds with the marshmallow and freeze. Scoop out the centres with a large Parisian scoop, and refreeze.

Make the sorbet by mixing all the ingredients together. Freeze and Pacojet or churn in an ice cream machine as normal. When set, fill in the scooped-out marshmallows and return to the freezer until required.

To finish the dish, remove the parfait from the freezer 10 minutes before serving. Place the marshmallow on top of the parfait and very carefully colour with a blow torch.

Al's advice
Another welcome addition is poached fresh strawberries in a light syrup. Add a touch of cinnamon and star anise, and allow to infuse overnight in the refrigerator.

Soufflé

Pistachio soufflé, apricot espuma, apricot sorbet

A soufflé is an integral part of the dining experience for some guests – light and elegant, a lovely way to finish a meal.

Serves 4

Soufflé Mixture

200g pistachio soufflé base

(see basics 115)

soft unsalted butter

and sugar to dust

8 egg whites

150g sugar

Apricot Sorbet

500g apricot purée

15g sugar syrup

10g lemon juice

Apricot Espuma

(see basics 216)

To finish

50g chopped

pistachio nuts

candied pistachio nuts

(see basics 217)

Preparation

The soufflé base can be made 24 hours in advance using the basic recipe.

Apricot sorbet and espuma bases can be prepared in advance and finished 2–3 hours before serving. The sorbet is made by combining all the ingredients and churning or Pacojetting in the usual way.

Brush four large ramekins evenly and thinly with soft unsalted butter and dust with sugar. Place in the refrigerator to set. Remove and repeat the process. Set aside.

To finish, whisk the egg whites to soft peak, then slowly add the sugar. Take one-third of the egg whites and mix into the soufflé base, ensuring that it is well mixed and smooth. Very carefully fold the soufflé base back through the remaining egg whites. Place the mixture in the prepared ramekins and cook at 180°C for 6–7 minutes. Serve immediately.

Al's advice
This soufflé mixture is quite stable so can be made up to 30 minutes in advance and then baked in the oven.

139

Pear

Poached pear in red wine, cherry clafoutis & yoghurt sorbet

Serves 4

Poached Pear

4 large Williams pears,

peeled

500ml water

500ml Cabernet Sauvignon

350g caster sugar

juice of 1 lemon

Cherry Clafoutis

(see basics 121)

Blackcurrant Jelly

(see basics 218)

Yoghurt Sorbet

175g water

22g glucose syrup

80g caster sugar

10ml lemon juice

50g whipping cream

125g natural yoghurt

To finish

blackcurrant sauce

(see basics 219)

fresh blackcurrants

picked mint

Preparation

To cook the pears, boil the water, red wine and sugar together. Lower the temperature to a light simmer and place in the pears. Poach gently until tender, then remove from the heat and allow to cool in the cooking liquor. Reserve in the refrigerator.

Make the cherry clafoutis and blackcurrant jelly and sauce, following basic recipes. These should all be made on the day you wish to serve the dish.

To make the sorbet, boil the water, glucose syrup and sugar and set aside until cool. When cool, add the lemon juice, whipping cream and yoghurt. Strain through a fine sieve, freeze at −21°C and Pacojet or churn in an ice cream machine.

To serve, remove the pears from the cooking liquor, gently warm the clafoutis and add the sorbet at the last minute.

Al's advice
The poaching liquor can be reused
Reduce the liquor by half, add a
dash of port and some crushed
black pepper, then gently poach
some waxy figs

Cones

Coconut ice cream, spiced nougat mousse & raspberry granite

Great fun as a little pre-dessert to tease the palate.

Serves 4

Plain Tuile

(see basics 126)

Coconut Tuile

(see basics 220)

Chocolate Tuile

(see basics 221)

Coconut Ice Cream

250g milk

75g whipping cream

100g coconut purée

4 egg yolks

90g caster sugar

10g trimoline

Spiced Nougat Mousse

60g egg yolks

80g caster sugar

75ml water

3 leaves gelatine

100g Italian meringue

5g spice powder (star anise, cinnamon and cloves)

450g lightly whipped cream

Raspberry Granite

75g sugar

175g water

40g raspberry purée

10g eau de vie framboise

Preparation

All the tuiles can be made following basic recipes. They are best made on the day you wish to serve them.

To make the ice cream, place the milk, cream and coconut purée in a pan and bring to the boil. Whisk the egg yolks and sugar together. Pour half the milk onto the yolks and whisk together immediately. Add this mixture back to the pan with the remaining milk. Reduce the heat and cook to 85°C, stirring constantly. Now add the trimoline, pass through a fine sieve and chill over ice. Freeze to −21°C and Pacojet or churn in an ice cream machine.

To make the mousse, place the egg yolks, sugar and water in a round-bottomed bowl, and whisk over simmering water until a thick ribbon-like consistency is achieved. Soak the gelatine in cold water until soft, strain well and whisk into the sabayon. Fold in the Italian meringue, then fold in the spice powder and cream. Set aside in the refrigerator.

The raspberry granite can be made 2–3 days in advance and kept in the freezer. Dissolve the sugar in the water, and add the purée and eau de vie. Pour onto a flat tray and freeze. When frozen, scrape with a fork to create small crystals.

To finish, work very quickly or the tuile biscuits will go soggy. Coconut ice cream goes with the plain tuile, spiced nougat mousse with the coconut tuile and raspberry granite with the chocolate tuile.

Al's advice
The list of possible fillings for the tuiles is endless. I prefer using different textures and temperatures.

Orange & Cola

Orange bavarois, olive oil cake & Coca Cola sorbet

Chef Will had an idea – he had it in his head! Lots of little bits we have run on our à la carte menu over the last three years. A little random, but tastes amazing.

Serves 4

Blood Orange Pâte de Fruit
(see basics 222)

Blood Orange Carpaccio
(see separate recipe on page 129)

Orange Reduction
(see basics 223)

Orange Bavarois
100g caster sugar
65g water
2 leaves gelatine
125g orange purée (Boiron)
125g lightly whipped cream

Olive Oil Cake
45g brioche crumbs
105g ground almonds
150g caster sugar
1 tsp baking powder
4 whole eggs
210g olive oil
zest of 3 oranges

Coca Cola Sorbet
100g whipping cream
40g caster sugar
10g glucose
300g Coca Cola
1 leaf gelatine

To finish
caramel stick
dried blood orange slices

Preparation

The pâte de fruit, carpaccio and orange reduction can be made following basic recipes up to 36 hours in advance.

Orange bavarois is best made on the day. Make a sugar syrup using the sugar and water. Soak the gelatine in cold water and strain well, then dissolve into the syrup. Whisk in the orange purée, and cool down over ice until thick. Fold in the cream and set in moulds.

The olive oil cake keeps really well – you can keep it in an airtight box for five days. Place the brioche crumbs, almonds, sugar and baking powder in a large bowl and mix well. Whisk together the eggs, olive oil and orange zest. Gradually add the liquids to the dry ingredients to achieve a smooth paste. Bake in a lined baking tin for 45–50 minutes at 110°C. Remove from the oven and turn out onto a cooling rack. Allow to cool, then cut into discs that will sit underneath the bavarois.

The sorbet is quite simple. Boil the cream, caster sugar and glucose syrup. Soak the gelatine in cold water and strain well. Add the hot liquid, whisk in the coke, then freeze to −21°C and Pacojet or churn as normal.

Al's advice
If you find this dish a little too intricate, the same basic recipes could be followed and you could do a nice layered presentation in a Martini glass.

145

Tiramisù

Mascarpone & amaretto mousse, white coffee ice cream, amaretto jelly

The basic recipe for the Tiramisù was given to me by Benoit Blin. A take on a classic, and one of my favourite desserts

Serves 4

White Coffee Ice Cream

(see basics 224)

Amaretto Jelly

(see basics 150)

Grue de Cacao

(see basics 225)

Chocolate Tuile

(see basics 221)

Mascarpone & Amaretto Mousse

70g egg yolks

100g caster sugar

2 leaves gelatine

25g whipping cream

250g mascarpone cheese

50g amaretto

250g whipping cream, lightly whipped

To finish

melted 58% chocolate

chocolate coffee beans

Preparation

Make the white coffee ice cream and amaretto jelly 24 hours in advance, following the basic recipes.

The biscuits and mascarpone mousse are best made on the day you want to serve them.

To make the mascarpone mousse, place the egg yolks in an electric mixer and whisk on a high speed while you cook the sugar to 121°C. Pour the sugar onto the yolks and whisk until cold.

Soak the gelatine in cold water for 15 minutes and strain well. Warm the 25g whipping cream and dissolve the soaked gelatine into it. Set aside.

Whisk the mascarpone until smooth. Fold in the amaretto, then add the gelatine and cream mixture. Fold in the sabayon, then add the lightly whipped cream. Pour into moulds and place in the refrigerator for 6 hours.

Allow to sit at room temperature for 5 minutes before serving.

Al's advice

This mascarpone mousse recipe can also be frozen in advance

'All great cuisines of the
world have a strong
regional and local
identity. They reflect
culture and religion
and can unite all
around the table!'

Chef Michael Caines

'As a chef I believe it is my duty to source and use the
best quality ingredients and give them the respect they
deserve by using and cooking them to the best of my ability.'
Chef Will Holland

'When I arrived in the Pommery Room
I felt straightaway that the soul and
essence of Pommery was floating in this
amazing restaurant that is L'Ortolan.
My senses have been fulfilled and
completely satisfied because each
dish that the chef, Alan Murchison,
prepared was born to befriend our
wines. An unforgettable memory, and
therefore a big bravo for this outstanding
gem of a restaurant, where our passions
have found a new home.'

Chef de Cave, Thierry Gasco
Champagne Pommery

Book people

Mark Law: we have known each other for over ten years. Mark and I have been working on the book for two years and have never had a cross word – quite an achievement! Mark is a very gifted photographer and a top bloke.

Julia Charles, nutritionist and lovely lady.

Lisa Foreman, my designer, for a beautiful layout and design.

Chris Hodgson at Arkle Print, for printing and publishing.

Rowena Moore, my PA, who has the impossible task of trying to get me organised.

Suppliers

Steelite International, for all the stunning crockery and stemware used in the book and in my restaurants.

All the team at Donald Russell, THE top gourmet shop in the UK.

Sara Hicks from Pommery Champagne, my favourite fizz by far and house champagne of choice.

Janie and John Turner of Thermomix UK. Thermomix is the best gadget to enter my kitchen, ever.

Eric Charriaux of Premier Cheese, in a different league to other cheese suppliers.

Carlos and Antoine Zentei of Valimex, for all things French, the finest fruit and vegetables and also lots of lovely truffles.

Kevin Bartlett of Top Catch, the smallest supplier I use with the freshest shellfish available.

Jerome Poussin of Bragard. He makes all my chefs look like the professionals they are.

huge thanks to...

Unsung heroes

Will Holland, my Head Chef and ginger brother. Will has been by my side on many a long day doing food photography – a bloody good job too!

To my kitchen team who have picked up the pieces and endured the pillaging of their fridges before, during and after service, allowing me to do all the food shots. Big thanks to Goose, who has kept the ship tight. Swaino, Lidstone, Bartoon, 'Le Grand' Plowman, Phil Fanning, Simon Jenkins (the 'J' unit) – you know the score.

Front of house team, who so often get forgotten: Abi Lloyd, my General Manager, who has kept it all together while I have been all arty; Ania Gniazdowska, my Restaurant Manager; Steve Nisbet, my Sommelier.

Dr Frederick Mostert, for all his invaluable advice and 'secret' supplies of pate negra.

Mike Murphy of Reading Audi, for feeding my car habit.

Richard Hemmington, for his faith and confidence and for putting his money where my mouth is!

DONALD RUSSELL

DONALD RUSSELL'S MISSION

To provide a complete gourmet experience
to people in their homes and their favourite
restaurants, using the best tasting natural
products which have been expertly prepared.

Donald Russell is above all committed to quality
and, through the skill and innovation of our
people, we deliver great customer service,
outstanding value and most importantly taste.

steelite
INTERNATIONAL

It is interesting to recall that the association with Alan arose from a simple request for information on a product that he had seen whilst on vacation. From this enquiry a subsequent meeting moved quickly on to food presentation, Steelite International's intent to present its broad portfolio of tableware products in restaurant 'lifestyle' format and a mutual desire for authenticity in imagery.

When Alan added 'I know a good photographer', the die was cast and the three elements have come together to form a creative unit which puts excitement and expectation on the page.

Steelite International is a market leading manufacturer and supplier of tableware to the hospitality industry, with sales reaching over 120 countries around the globe.

Its close association with the restaurant industry is clearly evident in the pages of *Food for Thought*.

'To be the hospitality industry's preferred choice for tabletop products, achieved through the combination of inspirational design, excellent quality and outstanding service.'

Steelite International

UK Thermomix

With Thermomix, our aim is to make quality food preparation and excellent cooking accessible to everyone, young and old, amateur and professional.

Cooking with Thermomix is fast, easy, healthy and nutritious. It's also great fun! For chefs, Thermomix is a reliable extra pair of hands and an opportunity to raise menu quality to another level; for the home cook, Thermomix is an opportunity to discover and develop the art of cooking and to make difficult recipes easy and successful every time.

At a time when so many people are conscious of what they eat, we are delighted that Thermomix will help you provide healthy, delicious food for your family, friends and customers.

Happy cooking!

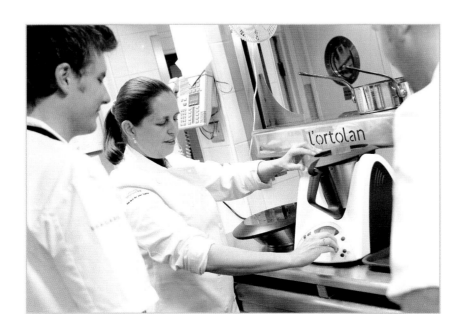

PREMIER CHEESE

Our passion for the last nine years has been to source farmhouse artisan cheeses from farmers, dairies and affineurs.

From Great Britain, France, Ireland, Italy, Portugal, Spain and Switzerland,we pick the best items, aiming to deliver them in prime condition. We also mature a dozen British cheeses in our Bicester premises, in order to present them with a maximum of flavour.

Cheese is simple, mainly made of milk, but complex because of its diversity. We work along with our clients to pass on some of our knowledge, making sure that when eaten, our cheeses will bring to the palate all aromas and flavours commonly found in traditional cheeses. Cheese is totally integrated in nature, and based on secular savoir faire and human skills. We simply want to keep up traditions and bring them into a modern world

POMMERY

All the great Champagne houses have created a prestigious universe of refinement, savoir faire and tradition: Champagne is the art of wine making and a special kind of 'art de vivre'.

* When you add the charm of 'avant-garde', Champagne becomes Pommery…

* Pommery is more than a luxury brand, it's a way of life

163

Quince Jelly
September 2006

basics

Basics Index

169

Basics 1
White Chicken Stock

1.5kg chicken wings
1.5 litres water
1 onion
2 sticks celery
1 leek
1 bay leaf
1 sprig thyme
2 cloves garlic

METHOD

Place 1kg of the chicken wings in the water and bring up to the boil. Skim and simmer for 45 minutes. Pass through a colander and add the remaining chicken wings and vegetables.

Bring back to the boil and simmer for 30 minutes, skimming every 10 minutes.

Pass through a fine sieve and reduce by half.

Basics 2
Brown Chicken Stock

1.5kg chicken wings
1.5 litres white chicken stock (basics 1)
1 onion, diced
2 sticks celery, diced
½ leek, diced
150g unsalted butter
1 bay leaf
1 sprig thyme
2 cloves garlic

METHOD

Place the chicken wings in the oven at 200°C for 30 minutes and roast until golden brown, turning every 10 minutes.

Place 1kg of the roasted bones in the stock and bring up to the boil. Skim and simmer for 45 minutes.

Caramelise the vegetables in the butter then pour into a colander to remove the excess fat. Add to the stock with the bay, thyme and garlic and simmer for 30 minutes.

Pass through a colander and add the remaining chicken wings. Bring back to the boil and simmer for 30 minutes, skimming every 10 minutes. Pass through a fine sieve and reduce by half

Basics 3
Veal Stock

1.5kg veal bones
150g plain flour
1 onion, diced
1 stick celery, diced
1 leek, diced
2 cloves garlic
500g button mushrooms
150g unsalted butter
500ml dry white wine
1kg canned plum tomatoes
2 sprigs thyme
1 bay leaf
1kg diced veal shoulder
1kg diced beef shoulder
250ml olive oil

METHOD

Place the veal bones in the oven at 200°C without any oil for 45–60 minutes, turning the bones every 10 minutes to ensure that they are golden brown all over. Sprinkle with the plain flour and return to the oven for a further 25 minutes.

Place the bones in a stock pot and cover with water. Bring to the boil, skim and simmer for 60 minutes, skimming every 10 minutes.

Caramelise all the vegetables in the butter until golden brown. Pour into a colander to allow the excess fat to drain off. Deglaze the pan with the white wine and reduce the wine by half.

Add the vegetables, white wine reduction, tomatoes, thyme and bay leaf to the stock base. Bring back to the boil and simmer for 30 minutes, skimming every 10 minutes.

Caramelise the beef and veal meat separately in the olive oil until golden brown. Pour into a colander to strain off excess fat. Add to the stock base and cook for a further 20 minutes. Pass through a fine sieve and reduce by half.

Basics 4
Venison Marinade

400ml red wine
200ml ruby port
1 carrot, diced
1 onion, diced
1 stick celery, diced
12 black peppercorns, crushed
1 bay leaf
2 sprigs thyme
8 juniper berries, crushed
2 cloves, crushed

METHOD

Bring the red wine to the boil and reduce by half. Allow to cool. Bring the port to the boil and allow to cool.

Mix all the ingredients together and pour over the venison loin and chopped bones. Allow to marinate for 12 hours.

Remove the loin and bones from the marinade. Reserve the marinade to use as a base for the bitter chocolate sauce (basics 154).

Basics 5
Duck Confit

1kg large duck legs
100g sea salt
25g crushed black peppercorns
2 sprigs thyme, roughly chopped
2 bay leaves, roughly chopped
3 cloves garlic, finely sliced
6 pieces dried orange zest

TO COOK
2kg duck fat, method 1 (traditional)
100g duck fat, method 2 (water bath)

METHOD 1 (traditional)

Mix all the dry ingredients together and sprinkle evenly over the duck legs. Refrigerate for 12 hours.

Scrape off the excess salt mixture. Cover the duck legs in the duck fat and cook in a low oven, 130–140°C, for 2 hours or until the meat is tender. Allow to cool, and refrigerate.

METHOD 2 *(water bath)*

Mix all the dry ingredients together and marinate the duck legs.

Scrape off the excess salt mixture and place the duck legs in a large sous vide bag with the duck fat. Cook in a water bath at 80°C for 12 hours, or until the meat is tender. Allow to cool, and refrigerate.

Basics 6
Soft Herb Crust

100g fresh breadcrumbs
50g grated Gruyère cheese
40g curly parsley
10g chopped thyme
5g fresh rosemary
70g soft unsalted butter
salt and pepper, to taste

METHOD

Place the breadcrumbs, cheese and herbs in a Thermomix or food processor and blend to a fine texture (speed 5 for 20 seconds in the Thermomix). Slowly add the butter on a pulse setting, and season to taste.

Tip the breadcrumb mixture onto greaseproof paper and roll out evenly until 2mm thick.

Reserve in the refrigerator until required. This mixture also freezes very well.

Basics 7
Tomato Fondue

500g onion, diced
5 cloves garlic, finely sliced
200ml olive oil
1.5kg ripe plum tomatoes, roughly chopped
2 sprigs thyme

METHOD

Sauté the onions and garlic in the olive oil until golden brown. Add the chopped tomatoes and thyme and cook over a medium heat until the mixture has reduced by half.

Use as a base for bouillabaisse jus and lamb jus.

Basics 8
Lemongrass & Galangal Jelly

4 leaves gelatine
500ml Sauternes
10 sticks lemongrass, finely chopped
2 kaffir limes leaves, roughly chopped
juice and zest of 1 lime
75g galangal, finely chopped
25g pickled ginger
50g lemon juice
sugar, to taste

METHOD

Soak the gelatine in cold water. Allow to soften, then drain and set aside.

Bring the Sauternes up to the boil and whisk in the softened gelatine. Add all the other ingredients and allow to infuse for 30 minutes.

Strain through a fine sieve and place in the refrigerator to set.

Basics 9
Fish Stock

1kg white fish bones, roughly chopped
1 onion, roughly chopped
5 cloves garlic
2 sticks celery, roughly chopped
1 bulb fennel, finely chopped
100ml olive oil
750ml white wine
250ml Noilly Prat
2 sprigs thyme
2 bay leaves

METHOD

Roughly chop the fish bones, removing any blood lines or skin. Place in a colander under cold running water for 1 hour, then drain well and set aside.

Sauté the onions, garlic, celery and fennel in the olive oil for 10 minutes without colouring, until soft. Add the white wine and Noilly Prat, and reduce the alcohol by half. Add the fish bones, thyme and bay leaves and cover with cold water. Bring to the boil and skim.

Simmer for 45 minutes, then strain through a fine sieve. Return to the heat and reduce quickly by one-third.

Basics 10
Morille Cream Sauce

500ml white chicken stock (basics 1)
75g dried morilles
6 shallots, finely sliced
1 clove garlic, finely sliced
100g unsalted butter
150g button mushrooms, finely sliced
250ml dry white wine
500ml double cream
salt, pepper and lemon juice, to taste

METHOD

Heat 200ml of the white chicken stock and pour over the dried morille mushrooms. Set aside for 30 minutes. Strain the morilles well, reserving the chicken stock for the sauce but being careful to discard the sediment.

Sauté the shallots and garlic in the butter for 10 minutes until golden brown. Add the morilles and button mushrooms and cook out for a further 10 minutes.

Add the white wine and reduce by half. Add all the chicken stock, reduce by half, and add the cream. Simmer for 15 minutes. Thermomix (speed 4 for 2 minutes) or liquidise until smooth. Pass through a fine sieve and season to taste.

Basics 11
Vegetable Nage

2 large onions
3 sticks celery
1 bulb fennel
1 large leek
2 whole heads garlic
100ml olive oil
750ml dry white wine

HERBS AND SPICES
3 star anise
12 black peppercorns
6 white peppercorns
1 sprig rosemary
2 sprigs thyme
3 bay leaves
12 pink peppercorns
bunch of flat-leaf parsley
bunch of tarragon

METHOD

Finely chop all the vegetables and sweat down in the olive oil for 3–4 minutes without colouring. Add the white wine and reduce by half.

Cover with water and bring to the boil. Simmer for 15 minutes, then add the herbs and spices and simmer for a further 5 minutes.

Remove from the heat and allow to infuse and cool. Strain and set aside.

Basics 12
Saffron Risotto

6 shallots, *finely chopped*
1 clove garlic, *finely chopped*
100g unsalted butter
250g carnaroli risotto rice
250ml dry white wine
saffron, to taste
500ml fish stock (basics 9)

TO FINISH
100ml fish stock (basics 9)
75g mascarpone cheese
freshly grated Parmesan cheese
lemon juice

METHOD

Sweat down the shallots and garlic in the butter for 3–4 minutes without colouring. Add the risotto rice and sweat for a further 2 minutes. Add the white wine and reduce by half.

Add the saffron, cover with 250ml of the fish stock and simmer for 15 minutes, stirring and adding extra stock as required. (Every different type and brand of risotto rice will absorb different amounts of liquid, so please use the stock measurements as a guideline.)

When the rice still has a little bite, remove from the heat and spread out thinly and evenly on a tray. Cover with cling film and allow to cool.

To finish, return the risotto rice to the heat, adding the stock until you reach the desired consistency. Add the mascarpone and season to taste with Parmesan and lemon juice.

Basics 13
Hot Smoked Sea Trout

1kg sea trout fillet, pin-boned and skinned
75g brown sugar
75g sea salt
zest of 2 lemons
bunch of dill
500g untreated wood chips

METHOD

Mix together the sugar, salt, lemon zest and dill. Spread evenly over the sea trout fillet and refrigerate for 12 hours. Scrape off the excess sugar and salt mixture and lay the trout on a perforated tray.

Place wood chips in a hot oven (220°C) for 1 hour. Remove and light the chippings – a blow torch is the best tool for the job.

Place the perforated tray over the chippings and cover with a lid. (At this stage the small flames should go out.) Allow to smoke for 15 minutes. Repeat this process two more times, or until you have the level of smokiness you require.

Basics 14
Braised Fennel

2 large bulbs fennel
white chicken stock (basics 1)
1 tbsp fennel seeds
2 star anise
2 sprigs thyme
2 bay leaves
1 cardamom pod, crushed
50ml olive oil
75g unsalted butter
salt and pepper, to taste

METHOD

Cut the fennel bulbs into four vertically, making sure that each piece still has the root attached. In a casserole dish, lightly colour the fennel on both sides. Cover with the chicken stock, then add the herbs and spices and season to taste. Simmer for 25–30 minutes until tender. (The cooking liquor can be reused.)

To finish, remove the fennel from the stock and dry thoroughly. Sauté in the butter until golden brown on both sides.

Basics 15
Dried Bacon Crisps
& Powder

smoked streaky bacon,
sliced 2mm thick
olive oil

METHOD

Line a baking sheet with greaseproof paper and brush lightly with olive oil. Lay the sliced bacon evenly onto the paper and brush lightly with olive oil. Cover with another piece of greaseproof paper, then place another baking sheet on top of the paper to press the bacon.

Place both trays and the bacon in a medium oven (140–150°C) for 35–40 minutes, or until the bacon is dry and golden brown.

The bacon can now be used as a

garnish or ground with a pestle and mortar for bacon powder.

Do not season at any stage as the bacon will already be salted.

Basics 16
Cauliflower Purée

400g cauliflower, finely chopped
500ml milk
30g butter
salt and lemon juice, to taste

METHOD

Place the cauliflower in a saucepan with the milk and bring up the boil. Simmer very gently for 35–40 minutes, or until the cauliflower is very soft. It is important that the bottom of the pan does not catch as this will affect the taste of the finished purée.

Pour into a sieve to drain off the milk, reserving 100ml of the milk to add to the purée if required. Place the cauliflower and butter in a Thermomix (speed 5 for 3 minutes), adding some of the reserved milk if required, or liquidise until smooth. Season to taste.

Basics 17
Curry Oil

10g garam masala
10g fenugreek
10g caraway seeds
10g ground cumin
20g turmeric
50g madras curry powder
6 cardamom pods, crushed
750ml olive oil

METHOD

Gently sauté the spices for 15–20 minutes in 250ml of the olive oil. Keep the spice mixture moving – if you allow the spices to burn the oil will have a bitter aftertaste.

Add the remaining oil and simmer for 30 minutes. Remove from the heat and allow to infuse for 12 hours.

Strain the oil through a muslin cloth, ensuring that the spice sediment is discarded. Store in the refrigerator and use as required.

Refrigerated in a sealed jar, this oil will keep for six months easily.

Basics 18
Dried Salmon Skin

1 large salmon skin, scales on
olive oil
cayenne pepper
salt

METHOD

Place the salmon skin on a chopping board scales side down. Remove any of the salmon flesh or brown meat that is left on the skin. Lay the skin out on greaseproof paper and place in the freezer for 6 hours. Remove from the freezer and cut into 10cm batons.

Place a sheet of greaseproof paper on a baking sheet. Lightly brush with olive oil and season the paper with cayenne and salt. Arrange the batons of salmon skin evenly on the paper and brush lightly with olive oil. Season and cover with another sheet of greaseproof paper. Cover with another baking sheet to press the skin, and place both trays and skins in the oven. Cook at 180°C for 12 minutes, or until crisp.

Basics 19
Hot Smoked Duck

4 large duck breasts
50g sea salt
25g crushed black peppercorns
4 star anise
zest of 3 oranges, dried in a low oven for 48 hours
500g demerara sugar

METHOD

Lightly score the skin on the duck breasts and rub with the sea salt and black pepper. Allow to marinate for 1 hour.

Scrape off the excess salt and pepper mixture from the duck breasts. Place the duck breasts skin side down in a non-stick pan, with no added oil or fat, and cook over a medium heat, without turning, until the excess fat has rendered down and the skin is golden brown – this can take 15–20 minutes. Keep the duck fat for cooking duck confit or roast potatoes. Set aside.

Grind the star anise, dried orange zest and sugar to a fine powder.

Line a roasting tray with a double sheet of foil and sprinkle the sugar mixture onto the foil. Place a wire rack on top of the sugar mixture, ensuring that the sugar is not touching the rack. Lay the duck breast on the rack and cover with foil, then place the roasting tray over a high heat. When there is a light smoke coming from the sugar mixture, turn down the heat and smoke gently for 8 minutes. Remove from the heat and allow to cool.

The duck tastes best when smoked and eaten within 24 hours.

Basics 20
Red Wine & Port Reduction

500ml red wine
150ml ruby port
150g sugar
juice of 1 lemon
juice of 1 orange
cinnamon stick
1 clove
1 bay leaf

METHOD

Combine all the ingredients and reduce slowly to a loose syrup. Do not reduce the mixture too far as it will set when refrigerated.

To test the syrup's consistency, spoon some of the mixture onto a plate and place in the refrigerator for 15 minutes.

Basics 21
Spiced Red Cabbage

1 large red cabbage, core removed
300g redcurrant jelly
150g brown sugar
2 tbsp five spice powder
3 Granny Smith apples, peeled, cored and finely diced
3 whole star anise
1 whole cinnamon stick
100ml eight-year-old balsamic vinegar
100g runny honey
2 tbsp crushed black peppercorns

METHOD

Slice the cabbage very finely. Combine all the ingredients and cook over a gentle heat for about 1 hour, until the cabbage is tender. Remove the whole star anise and cinnamon stick when cooked.

Basics 22
Tempura Batter

300g plain flour
200g cornflour
100g baking powder
ice-cold water

METHOD

Mix all the dry ingredients together and reserve. Add ice-cold water to the required amount of dry mixture to achieve a coating consistency.

Basics 23
Curry Tempura Batter

280g plain flour
200g cornflour
100g baking powder
40g Madras curry powder
10g cumin powder
ice-cold water

METHOD

Mix all the dry ingredients together and reserve. Add ice-cold water to the required amount of dry mixture to achieve a coating consistency.

Basics 24
Tapenade

250g black olives, stoned
2 cloves garlic
50ml extra virgin olive oil
6 anchovy fillets

METHOD

Blitz all the ingredients together in a Thermomix (speed 4 for 10 minutes) or in a food processor until smooth. Reserve in the refrigerator in a sealed container.

Basics 25
Truffle Vinaigrette

150ml olive oil
50ml white wine vinegar
25ml white truffle oil
50g truffle bouillon
20g chopped black truffle
salt and pepper, to taste

METHOD

Whisk the olive oil, white wine vinegar, truffle oil and bouillon together in a bowl. Add the chopped truffle and season to taste.

Basics 26
Oyster Vinaigrette

8 medium native oysters
25ml Cabernet Sauvignon vinegar or red wine vinegar
50ml groundnut oil
salt and pepper, to taste

METHOD

Dry the oysters on kitchen paper to remove excess water. Place the oysters, vinegar and oil in a food processor and blend until smooth. Pass through a fine sieve.

Make the dressing on the day you want to use it.

Basics 27
Hazelnut Dressing

200ml hazelnut oil
75ml white wine vinegar
50ml groundnut oil
salt and pepper, to taste
75g peeled toasted hazelnuts, crushed

METHOD

Whisk all the wet ingredients together and season to taste.

Add the toasted nuts at the last minute.

Basics 28
Horseradish & Potato Mousse

450g ratte potatoes, peeled and washed
4 leaves gelatine
100ml milk
450ml whipping cream
250g crème fraîche
75g horseradish relish
salt and pepper, to taste

METHOD

Cook the potatoes in salted water until soft. Strain well and set aside.

Soften the gelatine in cold water. Drain well and set aside.

Bring the milk and 150ml of the whipping cream to the boil and whisk in the softened gelatine.

Place the potatoes, crème fraiche, horseradish relish and gelatine mixture in a Thermomix (speed 5 for 3 minutes) or place in a food processor and blitz until smooth. Pass through a fine sieve.

Lightly whip the remaining cream and fold lightly into the potato mixture. Season to taste and refrigerate.Do not allow the potato mixture to get too cold as it will set and you will find it difficult to add the whipped cream

Basics 29
Horseradish Cream

200g horseradish relish
100g crème fraîche
salt, pepper and lemon juice, to taste

METHOD

Blend the horseradish and crème fraîche together until smooth. Season to taste

Basics 30
Bouillabaisse Dressing

200ml bouillabaisse jus
100ml extra virgin olive oil
10ml white wine vinegar
1 clove garlic, finely chopped
saffron strands, to taste
lemon juice and cayenne pepper, to taste

METHOD

Gently warm the bouillabaisse jus. Blend all the ingredients together until emulsified. Season to taste.

Basics 31
Tomato Consommé

2kg very ripe vine tomatoes

2 sticks celery, finely chopped
3 shallots, finely sliced
1 bulb fennel
2 cloves garlic
1 sprig thyme
2 sprigs tarragon
bunch of basil
dash of Worcester sauce
dash of Tabasco sauce
salt, sugar and pepper, to taste

METHOD

Blend all the ingredients together, making sure that the mixture is not too smooth: you are looking for a coarse dice effect.

Place in the refrigerator in a non-metal container and allow the flavours to infuse for 4 hours.

Hang overnight in the refrigerator in a muslin cloth. Correct seasoning.

Basics 32
Lamb Jus

1 kg lamb bones, coarsely chopped
750ml dry white wine
2 large onions, finely chopped
6 cloves garlic
150g unsalted butter
10 very ripe vine tomatoes, chopped
1 litre white chicken stock (basics 1)
1 litre brown chicken stock (basics 2)
6 sprigs rosemary

TO REFRESH SAUCE
200g roasted lamb bones
2 ripe vine tomatoes, chopped
1 clove garlic crushed
2 sprigs rosemary
1 sprig thyme

METHOD

In a large roasting tray, roast the lamb bones in the oven at 200°C with no added fat for 30–40 minutes, turning every 10 minutes to ensure they are golden brown. Pour into a colander to strain off any excess fat. Reserve 200g of the lamb bones to refresh the sauce later. Deglaze the roasting tray with 200ml of the white wine; set the juices aside.

Sauté the onions and garlic in the butter until golden brown. Add the tomatoes and cook until the mixture has reduced by half, then add the white wine and reduce by half.

Add the lamb bones, chicken stocks and herbs to the tomato mixture and bring to the boil. Skim and simmer for 50 minutes, skimming every 10 minutes.

Pass through a coarse sieve and reduce by one-third very quickly.

Add the reserved lamb bones, fresh tomatoes, garlic and herbs. Bring to the boil, skim and simmer for 10 minutes. Pass through a fine sieve and season to taste.

Basics 33
Red Wine Sauce

300g sliced onions
150ml olive oil
100g unsalted butter
250g sliced button mushrooms
50ml red wine vinegar
6 black peppercorns
2 sprigs thyme
2 bay leaves
1 litre full-bodied red wine
500ml white chicken stock (basics 1)
1 litre brown chicken stock (basics 2)
salt and pepper, to taste

METHOD

Over a medium heat, caramelise the onions in the butter and olive oil. When golden brown, add the sliced mushrooms and cook for a further 5 minutes. Pour the onion and mushroom mixture into a sieve to strain off any excess fat. Return to the pan.

Add the red wine vinegar and reduce by half, then add the black peppercorns, thyme, bay leaves and red wine and reduce by half again. Add the chicken stocks and reduce by two-thirds. Pass through a fine sieve, return to the heat and reduce to a sauce consistency.

Check seasoning. If your sauce is still rather acidic, add a little cream and butter to mellow it.

Basics 34
Tomato Jelly

1kg cherry vine tomatoes
1 stick celery, roughly chopped
2 shallots, finely chopped
1 clove garlic
1 sprig thyme
25g tarragon
75g basil
5ml Worcester sauce
dash of Tabasco sauce
salt and sugar, to taste

METHOD

Place all the ingredients in a liquidiser and blitz until smooth. Put in the refrigerator and allow to marinate for 3 hours.

Hang in a muslin cloth and allow to drip through slowly overnight. Correct seasoning.

Basics 35
Bloody Mary Sorbet

100g onions, finely chopped
75ml olive oil
1kg plum tomatoes, chopped
250ml tomato juice
100ml stock syrup (basics 178)
10ml white wine vinegar
75ml vodka
dash of Tabasco sauce
dash of Worcester sauce
celery salt, to taste

METHOD

Sweat the onions in the olive oil until soft. Add the tomatoes and cook out until the mixture has reduced in quantity by half. Allow to cool.

Blend the tomato mixture with the tomato juice, stock syrup, vinegar and vodka. Pass through a fine sieve and season to taste with the Tabasco and Worcester sauces and celery salt.

Churn in an ice cream machine and reserve.

Basics 36
Pickled Shallots

1kg large banana shallots, peeled, roots on
500ml olive oil
300ml red wine vinegar
200ml water
2 sprigs thyme
3 bay leaves
salt and sugar, to taste

METHOD

Slice the shallots into 30mm thick slices. Press out the small inner pieces and use for stocks/sauces. Place the large discs of shallots in a casserole dish and set aside.

In a saucepan, mix the olive oil, red wine vinegar, water, thyme and bay leaves. Bring to the boil and season well with the salt and sugar to create a sweet and sour effect.

Pour the olive oil/red wine vinegar liquor over the shallots and cover with cling film. Place in the refrigerator for 48 hours to allow all the flavours to infuse.

If the shallots are kept covered in the olive oil mixture in an airtight jar in the refrigerator, they should keep for 4–6 weeks easily.

The liquor can also be used as a dressing.

Basics 37
Avocado Purée

2 avocados, peeled and stoned
juice of 2 limes
60ml water
100ml olive oil
1 medium green chilli, deseeded and finely chopped
bunch of coriander, finely chopped
2 large spring onions, finely chopped
1 large shallot, finely chopped
salt and pepper, to taste

METHOD

Place half the avocado flesh in a Thermomix. Add the lime juice, water and olive oil and blend until smooth. Empty the smooth mixture into a bowl.

Finely chop the remaining avocado and stir into the smooth mixture. Add the chilli, coriander, spring onions and shallots, season to taste and serve immediately.

Basics 38
Lemon Oil Dressing

200ml fresh lemon juice
250ml olive oil
250ml groundnut oil
50ml white wine vinegar
grated zest of 2 lemons
salt and sugar, to taste

METHOD

Combine all the ingredients together in a Thermomix or food processor. Blend and season to taste. Keep in the refrigerator for up to 48 hours.

Basics 39
Cooked Beetroot

1kg large beetroot
5 litres water
750ml red wine vinegar
3 sprigs thyme
3 bay leaves
salt and sugar, to taste

METHOD

Peel the beetroot and place in a large saucepan. Cover with the water and red wine vinegar, add the thyme and bay leaves, and bring to the boil. Season with the salt and sugar. It is very important that the cooking liquor is correctly seasoned at this stage as the liquor will penetrate the beetroot. Simmer gently for 30–40 minutes, until tender. Allow to cool in the liquor.

The cooking time varies greatly depending on the size of the beetroot. Apple-size beets should take 30–40 minutes.

Basics 40
Beetroot Purée

500g cooked beetroot (basics 39)
1 litre beetroot cooking liquor
salt and sugar, to taste

METHOD

Remove the beetroot from the cooking liquor, chop finely and place in a medium saucepan. Cover with the cooking liquor and simmer for 30 minutes, until the beetroot is very soft. Strain off the cooking liquor and reserve.

Place the cooked beetroot in a Thermomix and blend until smooth, adding some of the cooking liquor if required to achieve a velvety smooth purée. Correct seasoning with salt and sugar if required.

Basics 41
White Truffle Cream Sauce

100g sliced button mushrooms
100g finely sliced shallots
250g unsalted butter
250ml dry white wine
500ml white chicken stock (basics 1)
250ml brown chicken stock (basics 2)
500ml double cream
50ml white truffle oil
salt and pepper, to taste

METHOD

Sauté the mushrooms and shallots in 100g of the butter for 6–7 minutes until golden brown. Add the white wine and reduce by half, then add the stocks and reduce by two-thirds. Add the cream and reduce to a sauce consistency.

Pour into a Thermomix or food processor and blend until smooth. Add the final 150g of butter and the truffle oil and blend until emulsified. Check seasoning.

Basics 42
Herb Crème Fraîche

250g crème fraîche
20g chervil
20g chives
20g tarragon
20g dill
salt and lemon juice, to taste

METHOD

Hang the crème fraîche in a muslin cloth overnight in the refrigerator to remove any excess liquid.

Finely chop all the herbs separately and mix with the crème fraîche. Season with the salt and add the lemon juice at the last minute.

Basics 43
Bouillabaisse Marinade

500ml extra virgin olive oil
12 star anise
zest of 4 oranges
8 sprigs thyme
6 bay leaves
6 sprigs rosemary
12 cloves garlic, crushed
24 black peppercorns
1g saffron strands

METHOD

Combine all the ingredients together and allow to infuse for 1 hour. Pour over the fish for your bouillabaisse and place in the refrigerator for 24 hours.

Basics 44
Confit Red Peppers

10 large red peppers
10 cloves garlic, crushed
6 sprigs thyme
1 red chilli
300ml white wine vinegar
3 litres olive oil

METHOD

Cut the peppers in half lengthways. Scrape out the seeds and discard.

Place the peppers, garlic, thyme, chilli, white wine vinegar and olive oil in a large pan and simmer gently for 10 minutes. Remove from the heat and allow to cool. Strain off the olive oil and reserve – the oil can be reused.

When the peppers are cool, peel off the skins and discard.

Basics 45
Confit Tomato

1 kg ripe cherry vine tomatoes
100ml extra virgin olive oil
salt and pepper, to taste

METHOD

We use confit tomatoes for a number of dishes. The principle is the same no matter what size or shape the tomatoes.

In small batches, blanch the tomatoes in boiling salted water for 10 seconds and refresh in iced water. Peel off the skins and arrange the tomatoes evenly on a non-stick tray. Sprinkle with the olive oil, salt and pepper and put into a very low oven at 60–70°C overnight, or until the tomatoes have reduced in volume by 50%. Allow to cool, then place in a sealed container in the refrigerator.

The object is to intensify the flavour of the tomatoes by the evaporation of the water within. If the tomato already has a good flavour, partially drying it will only make things better.

Basics 46
Wasabi Yoghurt

100g natural yoghurt
wasabi paste
lime juice
salt and cayenne pepper, to taste

METHOD

Combine all the ingredients together and season.

Basics 47
Spiced Figs

12 large ripe purple figs
1 litre light stock syrup (basics 178)
200ml red wine
100ml ruby port
2 cinnamon sticks, broken in half
6 whole star anise
1 sprig thyme
12 black peppercorns, crushed
3 cloves
1 vanilla pod, cut lengthways and seeds scraped out

METHOD

Trim off any excess stalk on the figs and set aside.

Place all the other ingredients in a saucepan and bring to the boil. Simmer for 15 minutes, then remove from the heat and allow to cool for 15 minutes. Place the figs in a kilner jar, and while the cooking liquor is still hot pour it over the figs. Place in the refrigerator and allow to cool. Let the figs infuse in the stock syrup for at least seven days.

The cooking liquor also makes a superb base for a champagne cocktail!

Basics 48
White Truffle Honey

250g runny honey
100g fresh Perigord truffle

METHOD

Finely chop the fresh truffle and mix into the runny honey. Put in a kilner jar and place in the refrigerator. Allow to infuse for at least two weeks before serving.

Basics 49
Red Wine Poached Pears

12 ripe comice pears
750ml red wine
300ml ruby port
1 litre light stock syrup (basics 178)
2 star anise
1 vanilla pod, split and seeds scraped out

METHOD

In a saucepan, reduce the red wine by half. Add the port and simmer for a further 5 minutes. Add the stock syrup, star anise and vanilla and bring to the boil, then add the peeled pears and simmer gently for 5 minutes. Remove from the heat while the pears are still firm to the touch.

Allow the pears to cool in the cooking liquor and marinate for 24 hours before serving.

Basics 50
Marinated Organic Salmon
for Sashimi Plate

1kg organic salmon fillet
50g wasabi paste
grated zest of 2 lemons
150g rock salt
150g brown sugar

METHOD

Mix together the wasabi paste, lemon zest, salt and sugar and rub into the salmon. Place the salmon fillet in the refrigerator and allow to cure for 3 hours.
Very carefully scrape off all the marinade. Slice the salmon very thinly and serve straight away.

Basics 51
Sesame Dressing

6 egg yolks
2 tsp wasabi paste
2 tsp soy sauce
150ml toasted sesame oil
150ml groundnut oil
juice of 1 lime

METHOD

In a mixing bowl, whisk together the egg yolks, wasabi paste and soy sauce. Mix together the sesame oil and groundnut oil and gradually whisk into the egg mixture. It is important that you add the oil slowly, as you would for a mayonnaise. When all the oil has been added, mix in the lime juice.

This is quite a large quantity of sesame dressing – it is nearly impossible to make a small amount.

Basics 52
Belgian Endive Jam

1kg white Belgian endive
600ml orange juice
500g sugar
15g picked thyme

METHOD

Finely chop the endive and place in a heavy-based pan with 500ml of the orange juice and the sugar. Cover with greaseproof paper and cook gently until the orange juice has evaporated and the endive has started to caramelise. Remove the paper and reduce all the remaining liquid. Mix the thyme through and finish with 100ml orange juice.

Basics 53
Carrot & Vanilla Purée

1kg carrots
500ml fresh orange juice
2 vanilla pods, split and deseeded
250ml olive oil

METHOD

Peel and chop the carrots. Place in a saucepan with the vanilla pods. Cover with the orange juice and a sheet of greaseproof paper and simmer for 25–30 minutes.

Remove the paper and reduce the orange juice by two-thirds. Remove the vanilla pods.

Transfer the carrots to a Thermomix and blend until smooth. With the machine running, slowly pour in the olive oil, allowing it to emulsify.

Basics 54
Braised Endive

4 large Belgian endives
1 litre white chicken stock (basics 1)
2 sprigs thyme
25g sugar
salt and pepper, to taste

METHOD

Gently simmer the endive in the chicken stock with the thyme and sugar for 8–10 minutes, until tender, and season to taste.

Allow to cool in the liquor.

Basics 55
Dried Orange Slices

1 large orange
100ml 50% stock syrup (basics 178)

METHOD

Slice the orange into 1mm thick slices on a gravity slicer. Brush with stock syrup on both sides

and place on a non-stick mat. Dry gently in a low oven at 80°C, until the orange starts to harden – this should take 3–4 hours. At this stage turn the slices over and allow to finish drying.

Basics 56
Orange Powder

1 large orange

METHOD

Peel the zest off the orange and dry in a low oven at 80°C for 24 hours, or until bone dry. Place the dried zest in a Thermomix and blitz to a fine powder.

Basics 57
Cèpe Powder

50g dried cèpes

METHOD

Dry the cèpes out for a further 24 hours in a low oven at 80°C. Place the cèpes in a Thermomix and blitz to a fine powder.

Basics 58
Lobster Mousse

1 × 500g native lobster tail
15g salt
1 egg white
2 egg yolks
350–400ml whipping cream

METHOD

Put a food processor bowl in the freezer for 20 minutes. Add the lobster, salt and egg white to the processor and blitz until smooth; don't allow the mixture to get warm. With the machine running, slowly incorporate the cream and egg yolks. Pass the mixture through a fine sieve.

Poach a little of the mousse in fish

stock to test the consistency and seasoning.

Basics 59
Vegetable Emulsion

2 litres water
30g salt
250g salted butter

METHOD

Bring the water and salt to the boil and whisk in the butter until it has emulsified.

Basics 60
Court Bouillon

3 litres cold water
750ml white wine
250ml white wine vinegar
4 bay leaves
12 black peppercorns
2 sticks celery, finely chopped
2 carrots, finely chopped
2 onions, finely chopped
1 head fennel, finely chopped
1 large leek, finely chopped

METHOD

Combine all the ingredients together in a large saucepan. Bring to the boil and simmer for 10 minutes. Remove from the heat and allow to infuse.

Basics 61
Fresh Mayonnaise

5 large egg yolks
10g white wine vinegar
10g Dijon mustard
500ml groundnut oil
salt and pepper, to taste

METHOD

Whisk the egg yolks, vinegar and mustard together. Slowly drizzle the oil into the eggs, whisking continuously until all the oil has emulsified and the mayonnaise is thick and creamy. Season to taste.

Basics 62
Lobster Dressing

500g chopped raw lobster shell
100ml olive oil
150g tomato fondue (basics 7)
100ml white wine
500ml fish stock (basics 9)
350ml mayonnaise (basics 61)
juice of 1 lemon

METHOD

In a large saucepan sauté the lobster carcass in the olive oil for 10–15 minutes. Add the tomato fondue and cook for a further 5 minutes, then add the white wine and reduce by half. Add the stock and cook quickly until the liquid has reduced by half. Blitz all the shells and liquid in a Thermomix for 30 seconds (very noisy!).

Press through a fine sieve, then return to the heat and reduce slowly until you have a thick liquid, being careful not to burn the bottom of the pan. Allow to cool then mix with the mayonnaise. Add the lemon juice to taste

Basics 63
Oyster Panna Cotta

2 leaves gelatine
200g oysters
225g mascarpone cheese
450g whipping cream
Tabasco and lemon juice, to taste

METHOD

Soak the gelatine in cold water for 10 minutes. Place the oysters, mascarpone and 300g of the whipping cream in a Thermomix or food processor and blend until smooth. Gently heat the remaining cream and dissolve the gelatine. Pour onto the oyster mixture and blend for a further minute.

Pass through a fine sieve and season to taste with the Tabasco and lemon juice. Pour into moulds and allow to set in the refrigerator for 2–3 hours.

Basics 64
Dried Lobster Coral

100g fresh lobster coral

METHOD

Chop the fresh lobster coral finely. Spread out evenly on non-stick paper and put in the oven at 80°C for 24–36 hours until bone dry. Blend to a fine powder.

Basics 65
Blanched Lobster Heads

2 live lobsters weighing approx. 800g

METHOD

Kill the lobsters by splitting their heads straight down the middle with a sharp cook's knife. Remove the tails and simmer for 2 minutes in court bouillon (see basics 60).

Trim the heads with a pair of sharp kitchen scissors until a nice clean dagger shape is achieved and save for garnish. Using a spoon, scrape any of the flesh that remains inside the head into cold water and bring to the boil. Simmer for 20 minutes. Place under cold running water for a further 20 minutes. Keep in the refrigerator and use as required.

Basics 66
Pomme Purée

2 large Desiree potatoes
250g coarse sea salt
50g butter
salt and pepper, to taste

METHOD

Cover a small baking tray with the salt and place the potatoes on it, making sure there is an even layer under each potato. Bake the potatoes at 180°C for about 1½ hours, until soft – the skin should not be too dark.

Remove the potatoes from the tray and cut them in half. Scoop out the cooked potato and pass through a fine sieve. Place the dry mash in a pan and beat in the butter over a low heat. Season to taste.

Basics 67
Bread Sauce

1 onion, finely diced
10ml olive oil
500g milk
7 cloves
7 black peppercorns
2 bay leaves
150g smoked bacon trim
1 sprig thyme
2 cloves garlic
1g nutmeg
400g fresh brioche crumb
salt and pepper, to taste

METHOD

Gently cook the onion in the olive oil until soft but not coloured. Infuse all the other ingredients except for the brioche crumb in the milk over a gentle heat for 30 minutes.

Combine the onions and brioche crumb in a bowl, then pour the milk through a sieve into the bowl. Mix well and season to taste.

Basics 68
Red Wine Dressing

300ml red wine vinegar
300ml olive oil
300ml groundnut oil
25g Dijon mustard
salt and pepper, to taste

METHOD

Whisk all the ingredients together and season to taste.

Basics 69
Dried Tarragon/
Coriander

12 large sprigs tarragon or coriander
dash of olive oil

METHOD

Take a large plate and cover it tightly with cling film. Brush lightly with olive oil then carefully place the herb sprigs onto the cling film. Microwave on full power for 60–80 seconds until the herbs start to dry out. Remove from the microwave and place above the stove in a hot dry place for 1 hour.

Basics 70
Red Pepper Powder

1 large red pepper

METHOD

Peel the skin from the pepper and dry it out in a low oven at 80°C for 24 hours, or until bone dry. Place the dried skin in a Thermomix and blitz to a fine powder.

Basics 71
Oyster Dressing

6 large native oysters
50ml Chardonnay vinegar
200ml groundnut oil
lemon juice, to taste

METHOD

Open the oysters and place in a sieve. Reserve the oyster juice.

In a food processor, blend the oysters to a smooth paste. Gradually add the vinegar, then slowly add the groundnut oil to create an emulsion. Season with a touch of lemon juice. Serve immediately.

This dressing does not keep well so make it and serve it straight away

CAVIAR DRESSING
Add 30g oscietra caviar and 30g trout caviar to the oyster dressing.

Basics 72
Gazpacho

3kg ripe plum vine tomatoes,
roughly chopped
600g cucumber, peeled,
deseeded and chopped
1.5kg red peppers, diced
130g onions, finely chopped
2 cloves garlic, finely chopped
12 leaves basil
50ml white wine vinegar
25g salt
70g sugar

METHOD

Mix all the ingredients together and place in the refrigerator overnight.

Place in a Thermomix or food processor and blend until smooth, then pass through a coarse sieve to remove any skin and seeds. Correct seasoning.

Gazpacho can be used as an easy alternative to tomato consommé or tomato jelly.

Basics 73
Jerusalem Artichoke
Purée

1kg Jerusalem artichokes
600ml vegetable nage (basics 11)
400ml whipping cream
salt and pepper, to taste

METHOD

Peel the artichokes and chop into even-sized slices about 1cm thick. Place in a pan and cover with the vegetable nage and cream. Bring to the boil and simmer until very soft.

Lift the artichokes from the liquor and put in a Thermomix.

Blitz until smooth, adjusting the consistency with the leftover cooking liquor. Season to taste.

Basics 74
Cooked Poivrade
Artichoke

3 lemons
2 litres water
5g ascorbic acid
6 large baby Poivrade artichokes with
long stalks
1 large banana shallot, roughly
chopped
4 cloves garlic
10ml olive oil
100ml white wine
50ml white wine vinegar
3 sprigs thyme
2 bay leaves
6 black peppercorns

METHOD

Squeeze the lemons into a large bowl and add the water and the ascorbic acid.

Start preparing the artichokes by snapping off the outside leaves as close to their bases as possible. Keep removing outside leaves until you reach the lightest in colour and most delicate inner leaves. Prepare all six artichokes to this stage. It is important to work quickly to prevent discoloration.

Peel the tough green skin from the artichoke head and stalk. Once the creamy white flesh has been exposed and there is no green left, submerge it in the acidulated water. Repeat until all the artichokes are prepared. Cut the remaining leaves away to just expose the choke.

Lightly colour the shallot and garlic in a little olive oil. Deglaze the pan with the white wine and the vinegar and add the herbs and peppercorns. Place the artichokes in the pan and just cover with the acidulated water. Season to taste. Bring to the boil and simmer for 3 minutes, then allow to cool in the liquor.

Basics 75
Horseradish Relish

1 stick horseradish, peeled and grated
50ml olive oil
1 shallot, finely diced
30ml white wine
10g grain mustard
salt and pepper, to taste

METHOD

Place the grated horseradish in a pan and cover with the olive oil. Heat very gently for 4–6 hours.

Put the shallot in a small saucepan with the white wine and reduce until all the liquid has evaporated. Mix the shallot, mustard and horseradish together and blitz in a food processor until the preferred texture is achieved. Season to taste.

Basics 76
Perigord Truffle Cream Sauce

2 large Perigord truffles, 60—80g each
500ml truffle bouillon
250ml white port
250ml dry Madeira
1 litre double cream
200g unsalted butter

METHOD

Gently warm the truffle bouillon. Roughly chop the whole truffles and place in the warm bouillon. Set aside.

In separate pans, reduce the white port, Madeira and double cream by half, then place them in a Thermomix with the truffle bouillon and chopped truffles. Blend quickly until smooth. Dice the butter and add gradually to the sauce. Season to taste – then perhaps try it again, just to make sure you have enough truffle flavour going on!

Basics 77
Herb Purée

2 large banana shallots
2 cloves garlic, crushed
75g butter
1kg baby spinach, washed and picked
1 bunch flat-leaf parsley, washed and picked
100g Parmesan cheese, grated

METHOD

Gently sweat the shallots and garlic in the butter without colouring. Add the spinach and parsley and cook for 5–10 minutes, until soft but not grey. Transfer to a tray and allow to cool.

Place the spinach mixture in a large conical strainer and press thoroughly; it is very important to get rid of as much of the liquid as possible. Put the spinach and Parmesan in a food processor and blitz to a rough purée. Season to taste.

Basics 78
Saffron New Potatoes

30 pieces turned ratte potato
1g saffron strands
3 cloves garlic, crushed
1 sprig thyme
750ml white chicken stock (basics 1)

METHOD

Put all the ingredients in a pan and simmer for 15 minutes, until the potatoes are tender. Allow to cool in the cooking liquor.

Basics 79
Rouille

8 egg yolks
1 medium potato, baked
1 clove garlic, crushed
pinch of saffron
100ml milk
60g lemon juice
300ml olive oil
salt and pepper, to taste

METHOD

Combine all the ingredients except the olive oil in a Thermomix. Blend for 2 minutes on speed 3, until the mixture is very smooth. With the machine running, slowly drizzle in the olive oil, allowing the mixture to emulsify and thicken. Season to taste and pass through a fine sieve.

Basics 80
Crispy Shallots

2 large banana shallots
20g cornflour
salt and pepper, to taste

METHOD

Peel and slice the shallots into very fine rings. Separate the rings and place on greaseproof paper. Allow to dry in a very low oven at 80°C for 24–48 hours.

When ready to cook, dust in cornflour and deep fry at 170°C for 2–3 minutes, until golden brown. Season to taste.

Basics 81
Glazed Salsify

2 long stems salsify, washed thoroughly
300ml red wine
300ml brown chicken stock (basics 2)
2 sprigs thyme
1 bay leaf
2 cloves garlic
50ml beetroot liquor
25g butter

METHOD

Peel the salsify. Place in a container and cover with the red wine. Leave to marinate for a minimum of 24 hours.

When the salsify has taken on a deep purple colour, remove it from the marinade and keep to one side. Pour the wine into a large pan and reduce by two-thirds. Add the brown chicken stock, thyme, bay and garlic and bring to the boil. Add the salsify and simmer for 5–10 minutes, until tender. Season to taste. Remove from the stock and allow to cool. Cut into 5cm batons.

To finish, place the salsify and beetroot liquor in a pan and reduce by two-thirds. While the liquor is simmering, slowly add the butter. Allow it to emulsify, coating the salsify.

Basics 82
Violet Potato Purée

1kg violet potatoes
100g butter
salt and pepper, to taste

METHOD

Place the potatoes in a large pan and cover with water. Season well and simmer the potatoes with the lid on for 30–40 minutes, until tender. Strain the potatoes and place in a bowl. Cover with cling film to retain the heat as you work.

Pass the potatoes through a fine sieve into a warm pan, peeling them one at a time so as to keep them hot while you pass them. If the potatoes become too cold they will turn gluey so work as quickly as possible. Over a low heat, beat the butter into the potatoes. If the purée seems dry, add a little more butter. Season to taste.

Basics 83
Glazed Blackberries

150ml light stock syrup (basics 178)
50ml crème de mure
100g fresh blackberries

METHOD

Mix the stock syrup with the crème de mure and simmer for 3 minutes. Remove from the heat. Add the blackberries and allow to cool in the liquid.

Basics 84
Cider Fondant Potatoes

4 large Desiree potatoes, peeled
500ml cider
125g butter
2 sprigs thyme
1 bay leaf
2 cloves garlic
salt and pepper, to taste

METHOD

Cut the potatoes into the desired shape, making sure they are all of even size. Place them in a heavy-based, high-sided frying pan large enough for them all to lie flat on the base. Add the cider, butter, herbs and garlic. Cover with greaseproof paper and place in the oven at 190°C for 15–25 minutes, until the cider has reduced and emulsified with the butter and the potatoes are soft.

If the cider has reduced but the potatoes are not soft, add a little more cider and return to the oven. Season to taste.

Basics 85
Chicory Jam

1kg white Belgian endive
600ml orange juice
500g sugar
15g picked thyme

METHOD

Finely chop the endive and place in a heavy-based pan with 500ml of the orange juice and the sugar. Cover with greaseproof paper and cook gently until the orange juice has evaporated and the endive has started to caramelise. Remove the paper and reduce all the remaining liquid. Mix the thyme through and finish with 100ml orange juice.

Basics 86
Roast Red Pepper Mayonnaise

3 red peppers
350ml olive oil
3 egg yolks
1 clove garlic, crushed
5g harissa (basics 100)
5g tomato purée
5g Dijon mustard
salt and pepper, to taste

METHOD

Quarter the red peppers and remove the seeds and stalks. Place in a pan and cover with the olive oil. Bring to the boil and simmer for 10–15 minutes until soft, then remove from the heat and allow to cool.

Put the yolks, garlic, harissa, tomato purée and mustard into a Thermomix and blitz. Remove the peppers from the oil and add to the Thermomix, then continue blitzing until smooth. Slow the Thermomix down and gently drizzle the olive oil into the jug, allowing the oil to emulsify and the mayonnaise to thicken and become creamy. Season to taste.

Basics 87
Chicken Mousse

300g chicken breast
2 egg yolks
1 litre cold whipping cream
20g salt

METHOD

Put a food processor bowl in the freezer for 20 minutes. Add the chicken breast and egg yolks to the processor and blitz until smooth; don't allow the mixture to get warm. With the machine running, slowly incorporate the cream. Add the salt, and pass the mixture through a fine sieve.

Poach a little of the mousse in chicken stock to check consistency and seasoning.

Basics 88
Onion Confit

1 large onion, finely diced
1 clove garlic, crushed
100ml olive oil
salt and pepper, to taste

METHOD

Place all the ingredients in a small pan and season to taste. Cover with cling film and cook very slowly until the onion softens and turns translucent.

Basics 89
Pedro Ximenez
Sauce

500g chicken wings, chopped
100ml olive oil
100g unsalted butter
100g chopped onion
100ml sherry vinegar
200ml white wine
300ml dry sherry
1.5 litres brown chicken stock (basics 2)
100g sliced button mushrooms
200ml Pedro Ximenez sherry
salt and pepper, to taste

METHOD

In a large saucepan, caramelise the chicken wings in the olive oil and butter until golden brown. Add the chopped onion and cook for a further 5 minutes. Strain off the excess fat. Add the sherry vinegar and reduce until almost dry, then add the white wine and dry sherry. Reduce by half.

Add the chicken stock, bring to the boil, skim and cook over a high heat for 25–30 minutes. Strain through a fine sieve, then return to the heat and quickly reduce to a sauce consistency. Add the raw sliced button mushrooms and the Pedro Ximenez sherry and simmer for 5 minutes. Pass through a fine sieve and correct seasoning.

Basics 90
Glazed Chestnuts

200g peeled chestnuts
2 sprigs thyme, picked
600g brown chicken stock (basics 2)
100g butter

METHOD

Place the chestnuts, thyme and chicken stock in a saucepan. Over a medium heat, reduce the stock by two-thirds. While the stock is boiling slowly add the butter, allowing it to emulsify and glaze the nuts.

Basics 91
Champ

10g curly parsley
10g Savoy cabbage
6 spring onion tops
1 recipe of pomme purée (basics 66)
salt and pepper, to taste

METHOD

Pick the parsley and finely slice the Savoy cabbage. Blanch and refresh both items and squeeze out any excess moisture. Finely slice the spring onion tops.

Gently warm the mash in a small saucepan and combine with the rest of the ingredients. Season to taste.

Basics 92
Horseradish Pomme
Purée

200g horseradish, peeled and grated
200ml olive oil
2 Desiree potatoes
250g coarse sea salt
milk
salt and pepper, to taste

METHOD

Place the horseradish and oil in a saucepan and bring to the boil. Simmer gently for 20 minutes. Remove from the heat and allow to infuse for 1–2 hours. Pass through a fine sieve, reserving the oil.

Cover a small baking tray with the sea salt and place the potatoes on it, making sure there is an even layer under each potato. Bake the potatoes at 180°C for about 1½ hours, until soft – the skin should not be too dark. Remove the potatoes from the tray. Cut them in half, scoop out the cooked potato and pass through a fine sieve.

Place the dry mash in a pan over a low heat, and for every 100g of dry mash beat in 25g of the horseradish oil. Remove from the heat and beat in 30g of milk for every 100g of dry mash. Season to taste.

Basics 93
Fried Parsley

sprig of flat-leaf parsley
salt and pepper, to taste

METHOD

Wash the parsley and dry thoroughly. Deep fry at 170°C, until crisp but still bright green. Drain on kitchen paper and season to taste.

Basics 94
Parsnip Purée

500g parsnips, peeled
1 litre milk
500ml water
100g butter
salt and pepper, to taste

METHOD

Cut the parsnips into quarters lengthways and remove the woody core. Finely slice and place in a large saucepan. Cover with the milk and water and bring to the boil. Simmer gently for 20–30 minutes, until very soft.

Remove the parsnips from the liquor and transfer to a Thermomix. Blitz until smooth then slowly add the butter, allowing it to emulsify. If necessary, adjust the consistency with the cooking liquor. Season to taste.

Basics 95
Butternut Squash Purée

1 large butternut squash
100ml olive oil
500ml white chicken stock (basics 1)
20g butter
25ml boiled cream
salt and pepper, to taste

METHOD

Peel and deseed the butternut squash and cut into even-sized chunks. Heat the olive oil in a large pan and caramelise the squash. Cover with the chicken stock and bring to the boil. Simmer until the squash is very soft.

Lift the flesh from the liquid and place in a Thermomix. Blitz to a smooth purée, then add the butter and cream. Season to taste.

Basics 96
Shallot & Onion Purée

2 large banana shallots, peeled and finely sliced
2 large onions, peeled and finely sliced
10ml olive oil
20ml Madeira
200ml brown chicken stock (basics 2)
40g butter
salt and pepper, to taste

METHOD

Place the shallots, onions and olive oil in a heavy-based saucepan and slowly caramelise over a low heat – this will take 1–2 hours. Deglaze the pan with the Madeira. Add the chicken stock and reduce by two-thirds. Transfer to a Thermomix and blitz until smooth, then slowly add the butter until emulsified. Season to taste.

Basics 97
Perigord Truffle & Madeira Jus

250g squab pigeon carcass, chopped
75ml olive oil
50g unsalted butter
50g sliced shallots
50g sliced mushrooms
100ml red wine
350ml dry Madeira
500ml brown chicken stock (basics 2)
100ml truffle bouillon
50g chopped truffle

METHOD

In a saucepan, caramelise the pigeon carcass in the olive oil and butter. Add the sliced shallots and mushrooms and cook for a further 5 minutes. Strain off the excess fat. Add the red wine and 300ml of the Madeira, and reduce by half. Add the stock, bring to the boil and cook out quickly for 15–20 minutes.

Pass through a fine sieve and reduce to quite a thick consistency – correct this by adding the truffle bouillon and the remaining raw dry Madeira. The truffle bouillon must not be cooked out as you will lose the aromatic qualities. Add the chopped truffle at the last minute.

Basics 98
JBR's Choucroute

120g smoked bacon
1 small Savoy cabbage
4 shallots, finely diced
1 clove garlic, finely chopped
5ml white wine vinegar
120ml dry white wine
60g butter
60g flat-leaf parsley, picked and chopped

METHOD

Remove the rind from the bacon and cut into 1cm thick rashers; cut these into lardons. Put the lardons in a pan and cover with cold water. Bring to the boil and simmer for 1 minute, then drain through a sieve and wash any impurities off with cold water.

Discard the dark green outer leaves of the Savoy cabbage. Using a small knife, remove the core and then peel the leaves from the head. Wash the leaves thoroughly in cold water, then cut them in half and remove the large vein. Bring a large pan of salted water to the boil and blanch the cabbage leaves for 3 minutes. Refresh the leaves in iced water. Remove the leaves from the water and drain on a cloth.

Put the shallot, garlic and vinegar in a saucepan and reduce over a high heat until syrupy. Add the white wine and reduce the liquid by two-thirds. Add the butter and whisk until emulsified.

Basics 99
Thyme & Juniper Gnocchi

4 medium potatoes, baked on salt
2 eggs
2 egg yolks
3 sprigs thyme, picked
8 juniper berries, crushed and finely chopped
100g fécule

METHOD

Cut the potatoes in half and scoop out the flesh. Pass it through a fine sieve into a bowl, then cover the bowl and keep warm.

In a separate bowl, mix the eggs, yolks, thyme, juniper and fécule until smooth, then combine with 300g of potato. Try not to incorporate too much air as you mix. Season to taste. Put the potato mixture into a piping bag and allow to cool in the refrigerator for 1 hour.

Lay a piece of cling film about 60cm long onto a flat surface and pipe a 4cm thick tube of gnocchi about 40cm long. Repeat this process until all the gnocchi mixture is used. Roll the cling film tightly around the gnocchi, trying to avoid air bubbles.

Pinch the cling film at the ends of the mixture and tie a knot to form a sausage with no air bubbles.

In large roasting tray, heat water to 80°C. Gently place the gnocchi into the water and cook for 20 minutes. Remove and allow to cool.

Basics 100
Harissa

7 red peppers
15 red chillis, deseeded
1g saffron
7g salt
160g tomato purée
4g cayenne
7g ground coriander

METHOD

Cut the peppers into quarters, discarding the stalk and seeds. Lay the quarters skin side up on a baking tray and lightly brush with oil. Place under a hot grill until the skin has lightly blackened but not burnt. Cover with cling film and leave in a warm place for 1 hour.

Peel the skin from the red pepper flesh, and place the cheeks in a Thermomix with the rest of the ingredients. Blitz to a smooth paste.

Basics 101
Couscous

120g tomato juice
120g white chicken stock (basics 1)
160g couscous
15g courgette, diced
15ml olive oil
40g harissa (basics 100)
10g chopped coriander
salt and pepper, to taste

METHOD

Bring the tomato juice and chicken stock to the boil and season to taste. Place the couscous in a large bowl and pour on the boiling stock, then immediately cover the bowl with cling film and leave to steam for 2 minutes. Stir the couscous with a fork to separate the individual grains, then re-cover and leave for a further 4 minutes. Stir again.

In a hot frying pan, quickly fry the courgette in the olive oil. Transfer to a tray to cool. Mix the courgette through the couscous along with the harissa and the coriander. Season to taste

Basics 102
Moutabal

4 large aubergines
1 clove garlic, crushed
10g tahini
35g crème fraîche
25g lemon juice
salt and pepper, to taste

METHOD

Peel the green fir from the outside of the stalk and score a line all the way round each of the aubergines lengthways. Place under a hot grill until they start to char and take on a smoky smell. Allow the aubergines to cool then cut in half and scrape out the flesh, trying not to take the fibres from the skin with it. Place the flesh in a Thermomix along with all the other ingredients and blitz until smooth. Season to taste.

Basics 103
Chickpea Salsa

240g cooked chickpeas, peeled
5g red chilli, cut into fine dice
4 very fine slivers garlic
1g coriander leaf, finely sliced
25g lemon juice
25g olive oil
2g sugar
salt and pepper, to taste

METHOD

Mix all the ingredients together and season to taste.

Basics 104
Ham Stock

5 smoked ham hocks, soaked in water for 12 hours
2 onions, quartered
2 sticks celery
1 leek
2 carrots
bunch of thyme
3 bay leaves
15 white peppercorns

METHOD

Once the ham hocks have been soaked in the cold water, rinse them well under cold running water for 30 minutes. Place in a large pan, add all the remaining ingredients and cover with cold water. Bring to the boil and skim, removing the white foam. Simmer very gently for 3–4 hours.

Pour off the stock and pass through a fine sieve.

Basics 105
Béarnaise Sauce

FOR THE REDUCTION
125ml white wine
125ml white wine vinegar
1 shallot, peeled and chopped
1 bay leaf
5 black peppercorns
3 tarragon stalks

FOR THE SAUCE
6 egg yolks
250g butter, clarified
10g shallot, finely diced
3 sprigs tarragon, finely diced
salt and pepper, to taste

METHOD for the reduction

Place all the ingredients in a pan. Reduce by half and allow to cool.

SAUCE METHOD 1
(Thermomix)

Put 25g of reduction and the egg yolks in a Thermomix. Set the temperature to 60°C and stir for 15 minutes until the eggs have thickened. While the machine is still running, very slowly add the butter, allowing time for the mixture to fully emulsify between additions. Remove from the Thermomix and fold in the diced shallot and tarragon. Season to taste.

SAUCE METHOD 2
(traditional)

Put 25g of reduction and the egg yolks in a metal bowl. Whisk over a pan of very gently simmering water; don't let the bottom of the bowl touch the water. Whisk continuously until the eggs thicken and they lose their raw taste. Continue whisking and slowly drizzle in the butter, giving it time to fully emulsify between additions. Squeeze the sauce

through a muslin cloth and fold in the tarragon and diced shallot. Season to taste.

Basics 106
Confit Shallots

6 long banana shallots
thyme
garlic
bay leaf
350g duck fat
15ml olive oil
15g butter
salt and pepper, to taste

METHOD

Place the shallots, thyme, garlic and bay leaf in a pan and cover with the duck fat. Bring the duck fat to 60°C and cook the shallots for 45–60 minutes, until just tender. Remove from the fat and chill. Cut the shallots into 2cm thick rings.

To finish, heat the olive oil in a non-stick frying pan over a medium heat. Caramelise the shallots on one side until golden brown. Add the butter, baste the shallots with the foam, turn and season.

Basics 107
Fig & Mustard Chutney

180g dried figs, diced
250ml water
15g white wine vinegar
15g crushed mustard seed
15g crushed root ginger
130ml white wine
2g cornflour

METHOD

Put the figs, water, vinegar, mustard and ginger in a large pan and bring to the boil over a medium heat. Mix the white wine and cornflour together and stir into the figs. Continue cooking for a further 5 minutes, then

remove from the heat and cool. Season to taste.

Basics 108
Quince Jelly

3kg quince
300ml water
sugar

METHOD

Wash and quarter the quince then transfer to a sealable bag with the water. Cook in a water bath at 80°C for 24 hours until very soft. Transfer the fruit to a muslin and hang over a bowl to collect all the juice; massage the fruit to extract as much juice as possible.

Measure the liquid, and for every litre of juice add 800g sugar. Bring this to the boil and cook to 104°C; hold at this temperature for 20 minutes. Pour into sterilised jam jars and allow to cool.

Basics 109
Piccalilli

1 cauliflower, in florets
3 onions, chopped
8 baby onions, peeled
35g salt
600ml white wine vinegar
300ml malt vinegar
red chilli, finely diced
350g sugar
50g English mustard powder
25g turmeric
30g cornflour
2 cucumbers, deseeded and diced
salt and pepper, to taste

METHOD

In a large bowl, mix the cauliflower, onions and baby onions with the salt and leave to marinate for 24 hours.

Put the vinegars and chilli in a large pan. Mix the sugar, mustard, turmeric and cornflour into a paste and whisk into the pan. Bring to the boil and gently cook out until the cornflour has lost its raw taste and the sauce has thickened.

Lightly season the cucumber and place in a colander, allowing the liquid to drain away. Mix all the vegetables through the sauce. Season to taste.

Basics 110
Walnut & Raisin Bread

500g white flour
500g brown flour
20g salt
5g sugar
40g fresh yeast
150g milk
300g water
60g raisins
60g walnuts, peeled
50g semolina

METHOD

Place the flours, salt, sugar and yeast in a food mixer with a dough hook and mix until the yeast has been evenly distributed. Warm the milk and water to blood temperature and slowly pour into the flour mixture until a supple dough has formed. Knead the dough for 7 minutes on a slow setting until soft and elastic. Transfer to a large floured bowl and cover both the surface of the dough and the bowl with cling film. Prove in the refrigerator for 12 hours.

Knock the dough back and knead in the raisins and walnuts. Roll the dough into a large cigar shape and place on a baking tray dusted with semolina. Spray the surface with cold water and dust liberally with flour. Bake in a hot oven at 220°C for 20–25 minutes until golden brown and the base sounds hollow when tapped.

Basics 111
Apple & Rosemary Jam

2kg Cox apples, quartered
200g water
sugar
pectin
1 sprig rosemary

METHOD

Quarter the apples, leaving the seeds in and the skin on, and place in a bag with the water. Seal the bag and cook in a water bath at 80°C for 24 hours, until the fruit is very soft. Hang the fruit in a muslin, collecting the juice in a bowl. Keep moving the fruit around in the muslin to extract all the juice.

For every litre of juice you collect you need to weigh 800g of sugar into a separate bowl. For every kilo of sugar you weigh you need to add to the sugar 10g of pectin.

Warm the juice in a large saucepan and whisk in the sugar and pectin until fully dissolved. Over a medium heat, bring to the boil and cook until you reach 104°C – jam stage. Keep skimming the foam that forms on the top as you go. Hold the jam at 104°C for 20 minutes.

Put the rosemary in a sterilised kilner jar. Allow the jam to cool a little, then pour onto the rosemary.

Basics 112
Confit Red Onion

6 red onions, very finely sliced
100ml olive oil
200g brown sugar
20ml crème de cassis

METHOD

Combine all the ingredients together and cook over a gentle heat for 1–2 hours, until soft and sticky.

Basics 113
Caraway Seed Biscuit

150g butter
175g plain flour
175g wholemeal flour
1g salt
30g brown sugar
1 egg
60g water
25g caraway seeds

METHOD

Combine the butter, flours, salt and sugar in a food mixer fitted with a paddle attachment until the butter has been incorporated and the mixture starts to look like breadcrumbs. Mix the egg, water and caraway seeds together, then add to the rest of the ingredients. Mix until a dough forms, but try not to overwork. Wrap the dough tightly in cling film and rest in the refrigerator for 30 minutes.

Roll out the dough between two sheets of greaseproof paper to a thickness of 1mm. Return to the freezer until set. Cut into the required shapes and lay on a non-stick mat. Bake at 170°C for 7 minutes, turning the tray in the oven halfway through cooking.

Allow to cool, and store in an airtight container.

Basics 114
Celery Salt Biscuit

150g butter
350g plain flour
1g salt
30g brown sugar
1 egg
60g water
25g celery salt

METHOD

Combine the butter, flour, salt and sugar in a food mixer fitted with a paddle attachment, until the butter has been incorporated and the mixture starts to look like breadcrumbs. Mix the eggs, water and celery salt together, then add to the rest of the ingredients. Mix until a dough forms, but try not to overwork. Wrap the dough tightly in cling film and rest in the refrigerator for 30 minutes.

Roll out the dough between two sheets of greaseproof paper to a thickness of 1mm. Return to the freezer until set. Cut into the required shapes and lay on a non-stick mat. Bake at 170°C for 7 minutes, turning the tray in the oven halfway through cooking.

Allow to cool, and store in an airtight container.

Basics 115
Pistachio Soufflé Base

1 litre milk
170g green pistachio paste
200g egg yolk
200g sugar
115g flour
15g cornflour

METHOD

Bring the milk and pistachio paste to the boil. Mix the rest of the ingredients in a small bowl. Pour a little of the hot milk onto the egg yolk and sugar mixture and whisk well. Return this to the pan and cook on a low heat for 5 minutes, stirring continuously.

Basics 116
Soufflé Mixture

320g egg white
80g sugar
160g pistachio soufflé base (basics 115)

METHOD

Whisk the egg whites to soft peaks in a food mixer, then slowly add the sugar. Continue whisking until the egg whites are firm. Whisk a small amount of egg white mixture

into the pistachio soufflé base to soften it, then gently fold the remaining egg whites through the base. Use within 5 minutes of mixing.

Basics 117
Peach Schnapps Espuma

350g white peach purée (Sicoly)
3 leaves gelatine, soaked in cold water
600g apricot purée (Boiron)
50g peach schnapps

METHOD

Warm the peach purée and whisk in the gelatine. Allow to cool, then combine with the rest of the ingredients. Pour into a pressurised cream whipper and charge with 2 shots of gas.

Basics 118
Apricot Sorbet

1.5 litres water
300g sugar
1kg apricot purée (Boiron)

METHOD

Bring the water and sugar to the boil in a medium-sized pan. Whisk in the apricot purée and chill.

Pour into an ice cream machine and churn until smooth.

Basics 119
Poached Pears

800ml blackcurrant stock (basics 132)
6 firm pears

METHOD

Heat the blackcurrant stock to 60°C. Peel the pears, leaving the stalks intact. Remove the cores from the base of the fruit using

a Parisian scoop. Submerge the fruit in the stock and hold at 60°C for 15–20 minutes, until tender.

Basics 120
Yoghurt Sorbet

350g yoghurt
450g 50% stock syrup (basics 178)

METHOD

Mix the ingredients together. Pour into an ice cream machine and churn until smooth.

Basics 121
Clafoutis

6 eggs
1 litre milk
200g sugar
50g almonds
200g plain flour
grated zest of 4 lemons
100g poached blackcurrants (basics 123) or cherries

METHOD

Mix the wet ingredients, then add to the dry ingredients to make a smooth batter, folding in the blackcurrants or cherries at the end.

Pour into a greaseproof-lined baking tin and bake at 165°C for 8–12 minutes.

Basics 122
Blackcurrant Pâte de Fruit

500g blackcurrant purée
100g glucose
535g sugar
15g pectin
8g tartaric acid

METHOD

In a large heavy-based saucepan,

bring the purée to the boil. Add the glucose and 485g of the sugar, and bring back to the boil.

In a bowl, combine the remaining sugar with the pectin and mix well. Whisk this into the purée and gently heat to 107°C. Whisk in the tartaric acid and immediately pour the jelly into a tray lined with greaseproof paper. As soon as the acid reacts with the pectin it will set.

Allow to cool for 2–3 hours at room temperature. When set, dust with a little sugar and cut into cubes.

Basics 123
Poached Blackcurrants

200ml blackcurrant stock
(basics 132)
100g blackcurrants

METHOD

Bring the stock to the boil and add the blackcurrants. Remove from the heat and allow to cool.

Basics 124
Cassis Sauce

300g blackcurrant purée
100g sugar

METHOD

Bring the ingredients to the boil and reduce by half to a sauce consistency. Pass through a fine sieve.

Basics 125
Wild Strawberry Granite

350g water
100g sugar
100g wild strawberry purée
50g wild strawberries, chopped

METHOD

Boil the water and sugar, then pour onto the purée and chopped strawberries. Transfer to a container and freeze. Stir with a fork every few hours until frozen. When finished, the granite should resemble coarse snow.

Basics 126
Plain Tuile

100g icing sugar
100g plain flour
100g egg white
40g honey
100g melted butter

METHOD

Mix all the ingredients except the butter in a bowl. Heat the butter in a small saucepan and pour onto the mixture, stirring until smooth. Chill until firm.

To cook, spread a very thin, even layer onto a non-stick baking sheet and bake at 150°C for 6–8 minutes.

Basics 127
Orange & Olive Oil Cake

8 eggs
390g olive oil
85g brioche crumbs
195g ground almonds
280g sugar
zest of 6 oranges
10g baking powder

METHOD

Mix the eggs and oil and pass through a sieve. Keep to one side.

In a separate bowl, mix all the other ingredients and then slowly add the oil mixture, mixing thoroughly. Pour into a lined baking tin small enough to allow a layer about 3cm thick. Bake at 110°C for 25–30 minutes.

Basics 128
Orange Mousse

200g sugar
130g water
4 leaves gelatine, soaked
250g orange purée
250g whipping cream, whipped to soft peak

METHOD

Bring the sugar and water to the boil. Whisk in the gelatine and pour onto the purée. Allow to three-quarters set, then fold in the whipped cream. Pour into a mould to set completely.

Basics 129
Cola Sorbet

600ml coke
100g sugar
25g glucose
1 leaf gelatine

METHOD

Boil 100ml of coke with the sugar and the glucose. Soak the gelatine in cold water until soft, then whisk into the hot coke. Add the remaining coke and chill. When cold, pour into an ice cream machine and churn until smooth.

Basics 130
Cola Jelly

300ml coke
50g sugar
1 leaf gelatine, soaked
cola sherbet

METHOD

Warm 100ml of the coke with the sugar, then whisk in the gelatine. Mix with the remaining coke. Line a small shallow tray with a double layer of cling film and pour in the jelly – it should be about 1cm deep. Allow to cool in the refrigerator until set.

Turn the jelly out and cut into the desired shape, then roll in the cola sherbet.

Basics 131
Confit Zest

6 large oranges
250g sugar
300ml water

METHOD

Peel the oranges with a potato peeler, removing any excess pith. Cut into fine strips (julienne), then place the zest in cold water and bring to the boil. Refresh, and repeat this process twice more.

Boil the sugar and water together to make a light syrup. Add the blanched zest and boil quickly for 10 minutes, until the syrup has reduced by half.

Any citrus zest can be used in this way

Basics 132
Blackcurrant Stock

1kg blackcurrant purée
700g sugar
2 lemons
500g water

METHOD

Bring all the ingredients to the boil, then pass through a muslin cloth. Chill.

Basics 133
Praline

500g fondant
500g glucose
300g sugar
200g hazelnuts, peeled

METHOD

Put all the wet ingredients into a heavy-based saucepan. Over a medium heat, boil until a golden brown caramel is achieved – this will probably take 15–20 minutes.

Stir the hazelnuts into the caramel. Pour onto a non-stick mat or an oiled work surface and allow to cool.

Break into 3cm chunks. Put into a food processor in small batches and blitz to a coarse powder.

Basics 134
Frangelico Jelly

250g Frangelico
5 leaves gelatine, soaked in cold water
vanilla pod

METHOD

Heat 100ml of the Frangelico and whisk in the gelatine leaves. Scrape the seeds from the vanilla pod and discard the pod. Mix the vanilla seeds and the remaining Frangelico into the gelatine mixture and chill until set.

Basics 135
Chocolate Crêpe Batter

40g cocoa
5g icing sugar
20g flour
50g sugar
2 eggs
1 egg yolk
75g whipping cream
115g milk

METHOD

In a large bowl combine all the dry ingredients. Add the wet ingredients and mix until smooth. Allow to rest in the refrigerator for 30 minutes.

Basics 136
Hazelnut Ice Cream

1 litre milk
50g milk powder
3 vanilla pods, split and deseeded
150g whipping cream
10 egg yolks
150g sugar
150g hazelnuts, peeled and chopped
150ml Frangelico

METHOD

In a heavy-based saucepan, bring the milk, milk powder, vanilla and cream to the boil. Whisk the egg yolks and sugar together and pour on a little of the hot cream. Return the egg mixture to the pan and, on a low heat, take to 82°C. Transfer to a bowl and chill.

Pour into an ice cream machine and churn until smooth. Fold in the hazelnuts and Frangelico, and return to the freezer.

Basics 137
Pulled Hazelnut

hazelnuts, peeled
fondant

METHOD

Lightly roast the hazelnuts. Remove them from the oven and gently push a cocktail stick into one side of each hazelnut, trying very hard not to split the nut.

In a heavy-based saucepan, boil the fondant to a medium caramel. Dip the hazelnuts into the fondant, being careful not to cover the cocktail sticks in caramel. Hang the dipped hazelnuts from a piece of polystyrene, allowing the excess caramel to drain away and their tails to harden. When cool, remove the cocktail sticks.

If they are not being used straight away, store in the freezer in an airtight container.

Basics 138
Chocolate Tart

680g double cream
720g 64% dark chocolate, broken in pieces
4 eggs
280g milk

METHOD

Bring the cream to the boil. Pour onto the chocolate and stir until melted. Mix the eggs and milk together and slowly incorporate into the chocolate mixture. Pour into a flan ring lined with blind-baked pastry and bake at 100°C for 45–60 minutes

Basics 139
Caramel Ice Cream

1 litre milk
150ml whipping cream
50g milk powder
150g sugar
10 egg yolks

METHOD

Bring the milk, cream and milk powder to the boil. In a large heavy-based saucepan, bring 50g of the sugar to a medium caramel. Remove the pan from the heat and whisk in the cream – be very careful as the caramel may spit.

In a separate bowl, whisk the yolks and the remaining sugar together. Pour on a small amount of the cream mixture, whisking as you pour. Return the egg mixture to the pan over a low heat and take to 82°C, stirring continuously. Remove from the heat and transfer to a bowl to stop the cooking. Chill, then churn in an ice cream machine until smooth.

Basics 140
Peanut Tuile

200g glucose
250g caster sugar
200g salted peanuts
25g butter

METHOD

In a heavy-based saucepan, bring the glucose and sugar to a blond caramel. Fold in the peanuts and butter. Pour onto a non-stick mat and allow to cool, then break into medium-sized chunks. Place in a food processor and blitz to a coarse powder.

Lay a sheet of silicon paper on a baking tray. Spread the powder out in an even layer and cover with another sheet of silicon paper. Bake in the oven 135°C until golden, then allow to cool and break into the desired shapes.

Basics 141
Tempered Chocolate Tear

300g 70% dark chocolate

METHOD

Over a pan of boiling water, melt the chocolate and bring to 53°C. Remove from the heat and work the chocolate with a rubber spatula. As you continue to work the chocolate it will start to thicken. When it reaches a heavy paste – 27°C – return it to the pan of boiling water and bring it up to 32°C. Once the chocolate is tempered, keep it in a warm place but do not exceed 35°C.

Lay a strip of acetate 60mm × 170mm on a flat surface and spread onto it an even layer of chocolate. Fold the strip in half, sticking the thin ends together to form the teardrop. Curve the teardrop slightly and place in a metal ring to hold its shape. Leave in a cool dry place to set.

Basics 142
White Chocolate Parfait

150g sugar
50g water
6 egg yolks
2 whole eggs
1 leaf gelatine, soaked
150g 29% white chocolate, melted
600g whipping cream, whipped to soft peak

METHOD

In a heavy-based saucepan, boil the sugar and water until 121°C is reached. Whisk the yolks and eggs in a food mixer until light.

Dissolve the gelatine in the syrup and, with the machine running, drizzle the syrup down the side of the bowl into the egg mixture, then pour in the melted chocolate. Continue running the machine until the mixture is cool and fluffy, then chill.

When the mixture is cold, fold in the whipped cream. Pour into the desired mould and freeze.

Basics 143
Bitter Chocolate Parfait

150g sugar
50g water
6 egg yolks
2 whole eggs
1 leaf gelatine, soaked
150g 64% dark chocolate, melted
600g whipping cream, whipped to soft peak

METHOD

In a heavy-based saucepan, boil the sugar and water until 121°C is reached. Whisk the yolks and eggs in a food mixer until light.

Dissolve the gelatine in the syrup and, with the machine running, drizzle the syrup down the side of the bowl into the egg mixture, then pour in the melted chocolate. Continue running the machine until the mixture is cool and fluffy, then chill.

When the mixture is cold, fold in the whipped cream. Pour into the desired mould and freeze.

Basics 144
Coffee Parfait

150g espresso
150g sugar
15 egg yolks
300g whipping cream, whipped to soft peak
20g Tia Maria
5g Camp coffee

METHOD

Boil the espresso and sugar until it reaches 121°C. Whisk the yolks in a food mixer until light and, with the machine running, slowly drizzle the syrup down the side of the bowl. Continue until the mixture is cool and fluffy, then chill.

Fold in the whipped cream, Tia Maria and Camp coffee. Pour into the desired mould and freeze.

Basics 145
White Chocolate Mousse

300g 29% white chocolate
120g whipping cream
3 leaves gelatine, soaked
600g whipping cream, whipped to soft peak

METHOD

Very gently melt the white chocolate over a pan of boiling water. Boil the 120g cream and whisk in the gelatine. Pour the cream onto the chocolate and leave to set in the refrigerator.

When set, whisk until smooth and then fold in the whipped cream.

Basics 146
Caramel Domes

600g fondant
200g glucose
50g nibbed almonds

METHOD

Bring the fondant and glucose to a blond caramel in a heavy-based saucepan, then fold in the almonds. Pour the caramel onto a non-stick mat and allow to cool. Break into medium-sized chunks and blitz to a fine powder in a food processor.

Sprinkle a 2–3mm layer of powder into a 10cm ring placed on a non-stick mat. Bake the powder at 170°C until melted.

Heavily oil two hemispherical metal moulds. Bring the caramel out of the oven and allow to cool just enough to handle – it should still be very pliable. Quickly work the sheet of caramel into the dome, with the edges overhanging. If the caramel sets before it is fully moulded, return it to the oven for 30 seconds.

While the caramel is still warm, trim around the top of the mould with a pair of scissors to form a clean edge, then immediately remove from the hot mould and place into a cold mould to set. Store in an airtight container.

Basics 147
Chocolate Sorbet

225g caster sugar
500g water
200g 70% dark chocolate
2 leaves gelatine, soaked

METHOD

In a heavy-based saucepan, bring the sugar and water to the boil. Whisk in the chocolate and gelatine. Chill.

When cold, pour into an ice cream machine and churn until smooth.

Basics 148
Cacao Tuile

600g caster sugar
200g glucose
500g butter
200g milk
10g pectin
600g grue de cacao

METHOD

In a heavy-based saucepan, boil 300g of the caster sugar with the glucose, butter and milk. Combine the remaining sugar with the pectin and dissolve in the milk mixture. Bring to 102°C, then pour onto the grue de cacao. Chill.

Roll the mixture between sheets of greaseproof paper until 2mm thick. Bake in the oven at 150°C for 10–12 minutes, then cool and cut into the desired shape.

Basics 149
White Coffee Ice Cream

60g coffee beans
1 litre milk
50g milk powder
150ml whipping cream
10 egg yolks
150g sugar

METHOD

Roast the coffee beans and add to the milk with the milk powder and cream. Leave to infuse in the refrigerator for 12 hours.

Pass the mixture through a sieve into a heavy-based saucepan and bring to the boil. Whisk the egg yolks and sugar, then pour a small quantity of hot milk onto the egg mixture while whisking. Return to the pan and very gently heat to 82°C, stirring continuously. Chill the mixture.

When cold, pour into an ice cream machine and churn until smooth.

Basics 150
Amaretto Jelly

250g amaretto
5 leaves gelatine, soaked

METHOD

Heat 50g of the amaretto and stir in the gelatine. Mix with the remaining amaretto and chill.

Basics 151
Blood Orange Carpaccio

250g blood orange juice
3 leaves gelatine, soaked in cold water
50g Campari
500g blood orange segments, drained well and juice retained

METHOD

Heat half of the orange juice. Mix in the gelatine and Campari, add the remaining orange juice and place in the refrigerator. Allow the mixture to three-quarters set, then fold in the orange segments.

Lay out a double layer of cling film, 60cm × 60cm, on a work surface. Place half of the set orange mixture in the centre of the cling film and form a sausage shape about 5cm thick. Roll tightly in the cling film and tie up each end. Freeze overnight until hard.

Slice on a gravity slicer, and place the slices back in the freezer until you are ready to serve. Remove from the freezer at the last minute.

Basics 152
Financier

100g ground almonds
50g hazelnuts
150g plain flour
300g sugar
1g salt
5g baking powder
400g egg whites
300g butter

METHOD

Place all the ingredients except the butter in a food mixer and beat very well until almost white – this will take about 20 minutes. In a small saucepan, heat the butter until it takes on a nutty colour and smell (beurre noisette), then allow to cool. Slowly pour the butter into the food mixer while it is running, allowing the butter to mix in thoroughly.

Butter and lightly flour the desired shape mould or ring and half fill. Bake at 170°C for 8–10 minutes.

Basics 153
Orange Ice Cream

MARMALADE
4 oranges, scored to the flesh twice around the circumference
1kg sugar
1kg water

ICE CREAM
1 litre milk
50g milk powder
150g whipping cream
10 egg yolks
150g sugar
50ml Cointreau

METHOD

To make the marmalade, place the oranges in a pan and cover with cold water. Bring to the boil and drain. Repeat this step another seven times – the more often you do this, the less bitter the marmalade will be.

Place the sugar and water in a medium-sized pan and bring to the boil. Stir until all the sugar has dissolved. Place the oranges in the stock syrup and bring to a simmer. Cover with greaseproof paper and leave on a very low heat for 6–8 hours, until the rind is tender.

Lift the oranges from the syrup and place in a food processor. Blitz to a coarse purée.

To make the ice cream, bring the milk, milk powder and cream to the boil in a heavy-based saucepan. Whisk the yolks and sugar together and pour on a little of the hot cream. Add the egg mixture to the pan and, on a low heat, take to 82°C. Transfer to a bowl and chill, then pour into an ice cream machine and churn until smooth.

Fold in 100g of marmalade and the Cointreau. Return to the freezer until set.

Basics 154
Bitter Chocolate Sauce

500g chopped venison bones
100ml olive oil
100g unsalted butter
50g chopped onion
50g chopped carrot
12 juniper berries
2 sprigs thyme
2 bay leaves
500ml venison marinade (basics 4)
500ml white chicken stock (basics 1)
500ml brown chicken stock (basics 2)

TO FINISH
50g 70% bitter chocolate, grated
2 juniper berries, crushed
50ml red wine

METHOD

Caramelise the venison bones in the oil and butter for approx. 10 minutes, until golden brown. Add the onion, carrot, juniper, thyme and bay leaves, and cook for a further 5 minutes. Pour into a sieve to remove the excess fat, then return to the heat and add the venison marinade. Reduce by half.

Add the stocks, bring to the boil, skim and simmer for 40 minutes. Strain through a fine sieve, then return to the heat and reduce to the required consistency.

To finish the sauce, whisk in the chocolate and add the juniper berries and red wine. Allow to infuse for 10 minutes, and strain.

Basics 155
Fondant

225g butter
230g 70% dark chocolate
175g sugar
210g egg whites
120g plain flour

METHOD

Melt the butter and chocolate over a pan of boiling water. Add the sugar and mix well, then remove from the heat and allow to cool a little – the mixture will not work if the chocolate is too hot when you add the egg whites.

In a large, clean metal bowl, whip the egg whites loosely. Fold the egg whites into the chocolate, then fold in the flour. Line the desired tian ring with silicon paper and pour in the mixture. Bake at 200°C for 8–10 minutes

Basics 156
Banana Ice Cream

500g banana purée
500g thick crème anglaise (basics 177)
125g crème de banane

METHOD

Place the bananas in the freezer overnight before you make them into a purée. Mix all the ingredients and chill. Pour into an ice cream machine and churn until smooth.

Basics 157
Caramel Sauce

250g sugar
450g cream

METHOD

In a large heavy-based saucepan, bring the sugar to a medium caramel. In a separate pan, bring the cream to the boil. Being very careful, pour the hot cream onto the caramel and whisk until incorporated. Reduce the cream until the sugar has dissolved and the sauce has thickened. Pass through a fine sieve.

Basics 158
Honeycomb

50g butter
50g sugar
50g brown sugar
100g golden syrup
5g bicarbonate of soda

METHOD

In a large heavy-based saucepan, bring all the ingredients except the bicarbonate of soda to 150°C – a blond caramel. Sift the bicarbonate of soda into the caramel and stir in. Pour onto a non-stick mat and allow to cool.

Basics 159
Caramel Mousse

160g sugar
110g double cream
2 leaves gelatine, soaked in cold water
45g egg yolk
250g whipping cream, whipped to soft peak

METHOD

In a large heavy-based saucepan, bring 125g of sugar to a medium caramel. Bring the double cream to the boil and pour onto the caramel – be careful, as the cream will boil violently. Whisk until incorporated, and then add the gelatine.

Whisk the egg yolks and the remaining sugar until smooth and creamy. Pour onto the caramel cream. Chill.

When the mixture is three-quarters set, fold in the whipped cream.

Basics 160
Banana Cake

500g soft bananas
500g sugar
4 eggs
50g black treacle
50g desiccated coconut
500g strong flour
1g salt
25g baking powder
100g milk
50g groundnut oil
200g 70% Valrhona chocolate, cut into small chunks

METHOD

Peel the bananas and seal in a plastic bag. Freeze and defrost. Freezing the bananas increases the flavour.

In a food mixer, beat the bananas and sugar for about 15 minutes. Add the eggs and beat for a further 5 minutes. Next add the treacle, coconut, flour, salt and baking powder, and mix well. Whisk the oil and milk together and slowly incorporate into the rest of the mixture. Lastly fold in the chocolate. Pour into a lined baking tin and bake at 165°C for 45–50 minutes until cooked.

Basics 161
Brandy Snap Tuile

500g sugar
250g flour
12g ground ginger
250g butter
250g golden syrup

METHOD

Mix all the dry ingredients. Heat the butter and syrup and pour onto the dry ingredients. Mix well and chill.

Roll into small balls and place about 10cm apart on a non-stick mat. Bake at 170°C for 8–10 minutes until they are dark brown and little pits have formed on the surface.

Basics 162
Poached Peach

6 firm peaches
1 litre 50% stock syrup (basics 178)
5g ascorbic acid

METHOD

Put the stock syrup and ascorbic acid in a medium-sized pan and heat to 85°C. Add the peaches. Bring the liquid back to 70°C and hold for 10–15 minutes, until the peaches are just tender. Allow to cool in the cooking liquor.

Basics 163
Vanilla Mousse

100g cream
50g sugar
2 leaves gelatine, soaked in cold water
250g thick crème anglaise (basics 177)
500g whipping cream, whipped to soft peak

METHOD

Warm the 100g cream and the sugar. Whisk in the gelatine and add this mixture to the crème anglaise. Chill the mixture. When cold, whisk until smooth and fold in the whipped cream.

Basics 164
Tuile Basket

100g icing sugar
100g plain flour
100g egg whites
40g honey
100g melted butter

METHOD

Mix all the ingredients except the butter in a bowl. Heat the butter in a small saucepan, then pour onto the mixture and stir until smooth. Chill until firm.

To cook, spread a very thin, even layer onto a non-stick mat and bake at 150°C for 6–8 minutes. As soon as the tuiles come out of the oven, place them on top of upturned moulds. Press a second mould over the top to form a basket shape.

Basics 165
White Peach Purée

200g white peach purée (Sicoly)
50ml peach schnapps
dash of lemon juice

METHOD

In a heavy-based saucepan, reduce the purée and peach schnapps by half. Add lemon juice to taste

Basics 166
Raspberry Purée

200g raspberry purée (Boiron)
50ml raspberry eau de vie
dash of lemon juice

METHOD

In a heavy-based saucepan, reduce the purée and eau de vie by half. Add lemon juice to taste.

Basics 167
Golden Raspberry Purée

300g golden raspberries
75g sugar
lemon juice, to taste

METHOD

Put the fruit and sugar in a heavy-based saucepan, bring to the boil and reduce by half. Liquidise and pass through a fine sieve. Return to the heat and reduce to the required consistency, adding lemon juice to taste

Basics 168
Bouillabaisse Jelly

bouillabaisse broth (see page 75)

TO CLARIFY THE STOCK
200g white fish (sole, plaice, etc.)
3 egg whites
1 sprig thyme
1 star anise
50g raw onion
50g raw fennel
5 leaves gelatine per 500ml clarified stock
salt and pepper, to taste

METHOD

Make the broth. Allow to sit in the refrigerator overnight and skim off any excess oil.

Place the fish, egg whites, thyme, anise and vegetables in a food processor and blend until fairly smooth. Whisk into the cold broth. Place over a medium heat and bring slowly to the boil, then allow to simmer for 15–20 minutes until the stock has cleared. Gently pour the stock through a double muslin cloth and allow to cool. Check seasoning.

Measure the liquid and soak the appropriate amount of gelatine. Heat 100ml of the stock and dissolve the gelatine as normal, then return to the base stock. Place a small amount of jelly in the refrigerator and allow to set; this will allow you to check the setting of the stock and also the seasoning when cold.

Basics 169
Passion Fruit Bavarois

375g sugar
260g water
500ml passion fruit purée (Boiron)
8 leaves gelatine, soaked
500ml whipping cream, whipped to soft peak.

METHOD

Bring the sugar and water to the

boil. Mix with the purée, then whisk in the gelatine. Chill until three-quarters set and fold in the whipped cream.

Basics 170
Passion Fruit Jelly

250ml passion fruit purée (Boiron)
25g sugar
3 leaves gelatine, soaked

METHOD

Bring the purée and sugar to the boil, then whisk in the gelatine. Chill.

Basics 171
Coconut Sorbet

225g sugar
500g water
50g trimoline
500g coconut purée (Sicoly)
40g Malibu

METHOD

Boil the sugar, water and trimoline, and pour onto the purée. Mix well and chill.

Pour into an ice cream machine and churn until smooth. Fold in the Malibu and freeze

Basics 172
Marshmallows

375 sugar
juice of 1 lemon
100ml water
190g egg whites
3 leaves gelatine, soaked

METHOD

Bring the sugar, lemon juice and water to the boil in a heavy-based saucepan. When the syrup reaches 118°C, start to whisk the egg whites in a food mixer. As soon as the syrup reaches 121°C, remove

the pan from the heat and stir in the gelatine.

The egg whites should have reached the soft peak stage by now, so with the machine still running, slowly pour the syrup down the side of the bowl and continue whisking until the mixture is cool. Spoon into the desired mould.

Basics 173
Wild Strawberry Sorbet

1.5 litres water
300g sugar
1kg wild strawberry purée (Boiron)

METHOD

Bring the water and sugar to the boil in a medium-sized pan. Whisk in the purée and chill.

Pour into an ice cream machine and churn until smooth.

Basics 174
Vanilla Parfait

30g water
75g sugar
1 egg
3 egg yolks
2 vanilla pods
300g double cream

METHOD

Boil the water and sugar until you reach 121°C. In a food mixer, whisk the egg and yolks until light. With the machine running, slowly drizzle the syrup down the side of the bowl and continue until the mixture is cool and fluffy.

Split the vanilla pods and scrape the seeds into the cream. Whip to soft peak and fold into the egg mixture. Chill. Pipe into the desired moulds.

Basics 175
Vanilla Ice cream

1 litre milk
10 vanilla pods, split and deseeded
50g milk powder
150g whipping cream
10 egg yolks
150g sugar

METHOD

In a heavy-based saucepan, boil the milk with the vanilla, milk powder and cream. Whisk the yolks and sugar together and pour on a little of the hot cream.

Return the egg mixture to the pan and, on a low heat, take to 82°C. Transfer to a bowl and chill.

Basics 176
Spiced Strawberry Sauce

500g strawberry purée
125g balsamic vinegar
5 peppercorns
3 star anise

METHOD

Put the purée and vinegar in a saucepan. Wrap the spices in a muslin pouch and add to the pan. Bring to the boil.

Reduce the purée by one-third and allow the spices to infuse for 30 minutes. Pass through a sieve and chill.

Basics 177
Thick Crème Anglais

250g milk
75g whipping cream
1 vanilla pod, split and seeds removed
4 egg yolks
60g sugar

METHOD

Put the milk, cream and vanilla pod in a heavy-based saucepan and bring to the boil. Mix the yolks and sugar together and pour about a quarter of the hot cream onto the mixture while whisking.

Return the egg mixture to the pan and slowly heat to 82°C, stirring continuously. Chill.

Basics 178
50% Stock Syrup

500g water
500g sugar

METHOD
Bring to the boil.

Basics 179
Vanilla Anglaise

150g whole milk
1 vanilla pod, split and seeds removed
2 large egg yolks
40g caster sugar
75g whipping cream

METHOD
Boil the milk with the vanilla pod. Whisk the yolks with the caster sugar, then pour half of the liquid onto the yolks and whisk together. Reboil the milk remaining in the pan. Add the yolk mixture to the pan, reduce the heat and cook to 86°C. Check the consistency; strain through a chinois.

Chill on ice, whisking for 2–3 minutes to release the steam. When cold, reserve in the refrigerator.

Basics 180
Sugar Syrup

1.1kg caster sugar
900g water
125g glucose

METHOD
Place all the ingredients in a

saucepan and mix well. Bring to the boil and make sure everything is dissolved. Pass through a chinois. Reserve until cool, and store in the refrigerator.

Basics 181
Sweet Paste

2 whole eggs
2 egg yolks
90g icing sugar, sifted
250g unsalted butter, softened
500g pastry flour

METHOD
In a machine bowl, beat the eggs and the yolks with the icing sugar. Slowly add the softened butter and beat in until smooth.

Fold in the flour gently, until fully incorporated. Wrap in cling film and keep in the refrigerator until required.

Basics 182
Sage Gnocchi

4 medium potatoes, baked on salt
2 eggs
2 egg yolks
100g fécule
10g finely diced sage

METHOD
Cut the potatoes in half and scoop out the flesh. Pass it through a fine sieve into a bowl; cover and keep warm.

In a separate bowl, mix the eggs, yolks, fécule and sage until smooth, then combine with 300g of potato. Try not to incorporate too much air as you mix. Season to taste. Put into a piping bag and allow to cool in the refrigerator for 1 hour.

Lay a piece of cling film about 60cm long on a flat surface and pipe a 1cm thick tube of gnocchi about 40cm long. Repeat this process until all the gnocchi mixture is used. Roll the cling film tightly around the

gnocchi, trying to avoid air bubbles. Pinch the cling film at the ends of the mixture and tie a knot to form a sausage with no air bubbles.

In large roasting tray, heat some water to 80°C and lay the gnocchi in it; hold it under with a wire rack. Cook for 20 minutes. Remove and allow to cool.

Basics 183
Tomato Pistou

8 large banana shallots, finely diced
1 clove garlic, finely chopped
2 sprigs thyme, picked
10ml olive oil
20g tomato purée
100ml tomato juice
100g sun-blushed tomatoes, puréed
25ml aged balsamic vinegar
salt and pepper, to taste
10g finely diced basil

METHOD
Place the shallots, garlic, thyme and olive oil in a heavy-based saucepan and cover with a tight-fitting lid. On a very low heat, cook for 1–2 hours, stirring occasionally until the shallots are translucent and soft.

Mix in the tomato purée and cook out for 5 minutes. Next add the tomato juice and reduce by half, then add the sun-blushed tomatoes and balsamic vinegar. Season to taste and cool. Stir in the basil.

Basics 184
Celeriac Cream

1 celeriac
1 litre milk
1 litre cream
50g butter

METHOD
Peel the celeriac and cut into small, even chunks. Place in a pan with the milk and cream, and bring to the boil. Simmer gently for 30–45 minutes, until very soft.

Strain the celeriac from the cream. Place in a Thermomix and blitz until smooth, adjusting the consistency with the leftover cooking liquor. Season to taste.

Basics 185
Pasta

500g '00' pasta flour
12g salt
3 whole eggs
10 egg yolks
10ml olive oil

METHOD

Put the pasta flour and salt in a food processor. Mix together the eggs, egg yolks and olive oil. While the machine is running, pour in the eggs; run the machine until the eggs are fully incorporated.

Remove the dough and knead for 5 minutes. Wrap in cling film and allow to rest for 1 hour.

Basics 186
Tapenade

200g black olives, pitted
1 sprig thyme, picked
1 clove garlic, crushed
5g lemon zest

METHOD

Place all the ingredients in a Thermomix and blitz to a coarse paste. Season to taste.

Basics 187
Basil Oil

4 bunches basil, picked
250ml olive oil

METHOD

Blanch the basil in salted water until the leaves turn bright green. Immediately plunge the basil into iced water. When cold, remove and squeeze dry. Place in a Thermomix with 100ml olive oil and blitz to a paste. If the basil is getting hot, place it in the freezer to chill before continuing. Add the remaining oil and blitz for 1 minute.

Pour into a double muslin and hang in the refrigerator for 3–4 hours, collecting the oil in a bowl underneath.

Basics 188
Basil Pomme Purée

250g coarse sea salt
2 large Desiree potatoes
basil oil (basics 187)
cold milk
salt and pepper, to taste

METHOD

Cover a small baking tray with the sea salt and place the potatoes on it, making sure there is an even layer under each potato. Bake the potatoes at 180°C for about 1½ hours, until soft; the skin should not be too dark.

Remove the potatoes from the tray and cut them in half. Scoop out the cooked potato and pass through a fine sieve. Place the dry mash in a pan and over a medium heat whisk in 50g of basil oil for every 100g of dry mash. It will look as though it has split.

Remove from the heat and slowly incorporate the milk until it forms a silky smooth mash, then pass through a fine sieve. Season to taste.

Basics 189
Guacamole

2 ripe avocados
70g red onion, finely diced
1 chilli, finely diced
5g coriander, chopped
10g lime juice
1 plum tomato, peeled, deseeded and diced
40g extra virgin olive oil
salt and pepper, to taste

METHOD

Cut the avocados in half, discard the stone and spoon out the flesh. With a fork, mash the flesh and mix in the lime juice, then add the remaining ingredients. Season to taste.

Basics 190
Pea Purée

250g frozen peas, defrosted
30g water
20g olive oil
salt and pepper, to taste

METHOD

Put the peas and water in a Thermomix and blitz until smooth. Slowly add the olive oil, then pass through a fine sieve. Season to taste.

Basics 191
Black Olive Salt

25g black olives, pitted
25g Maldon sea salt

METHOD

Dry the olives on a piece of greaseproof paper in a very low oven (80°C) for 24 hours, until bone dry. Put the salt and olives in a Thermomix and blitz to a powder.

Basics 192
Braised Baby Fennel

4 medium baby fennel
500ml water
2 star anise
10g fennel seed
2 juniper berries
5 black peppercorns
3 sprigs thyme
3 cloves garlic

METHOD

Trim the fennel and place the tops

in a pan. Cover with water and add the remaining ingredients. Simmer gently for 45 minutes.

Pass the stock through a fine sieve into a clean pan and bring it up to 80°C. Add the fennel and hold at 80°C for 50mins. Allow the fennel to cool in the stock.

Basics 193
Confit Baby Aubergine

4 baby aubergines
1 litre olive oil
2 cloves garlic
2 sprigs thymes
2 bay leaves
salt and pepper, to taste

METHOD

Remove the green fur from the stalks and peel the baby aubergines. In a deep medium-sized pan, heat the olive oil to 150°C. Carefully add the aubergines, and turn gently until they take on a slight golden colour. Reduce the temperature to 120°C and add the remaining ingredients. Cook for 8–10 minutes, until tender.

Lift from the oil and place on absorbent paper. Season heavily.

Basics 194
Confit Garlic

4 cloves garlic
250ml olive oil
1 sprig thyme
1 bay leaf
salt and pepper, to taste

METHOD

Place the garlic in a small pan and cover with cold water. Bring to the boil and drain. Repeat this process twice more.

Cover the blanched garlic with olive oil, bring to 70°C and cook for 20–25 minutes, until tender. Season to taste. Allow to cool in the oil.

Basics 195
Rabbit Farce

100g rabbit fat
100g rabbit meat
150g duxelles (basics 202)
5g Dijon mustard
10g chopped herbs (parsley, chervil, tarragon)
salt and pepper, to taste

METHOD

Mince the rabbit fat and meat through the mincing attachment of a food mixer, then add the remaining ingredients. Season to taste.

Fry a little piece to check the seasoning and adjust if necessary.

Basics 196
Carrot Purée

500g carrot tops, peeled and finely chopped
60g butter
salt and pepper, to taste

METHOD

Place the carrots and 25g of the butter in a heavy-based saucepan. Cover with cling film and cook very gently for 1–2 hours, until tender.

Transfer the carrots to a Thermomix and blitz until smooth, then slowly add the remaining butter. Season to taste and adjust the consistency with water.

Basics 197
Confit Rabbit legs

1kg rabbit legs
100g sea salt
25g black peppercorns, crushed
2 sprigs thyme, roughly chopped
2 bay leaves, roughly chopped
6 pieces orange zest

TO COOK
2kg duck fat, method 1 (traditional)
100g duck fat, method 2 (water bath)

METHOD 1 *(traditional)*

Mix all the dry ingredients and sprinkle over the rabbit legs. Refrigerate for 12 hours.

Scrape off the excess salt mixture, cover the legs with duck fat and cook in a low oven at 130–140°C for 2 hours, or until the meat is tender. Allow to cool and refrigerate.

METHOD 2 *(water bath)*

Mix all the dry ingredients and sprinkle over the rabbit legs. Refrigerate for 12 hours.

Scrape off the excess salt mixture and place the rabbit legs in a sous vide bag with the duck fat. Cook in a water bath at 80°C for 12 hours, or until the meat is tender, then allow to cool and refrigerate.

Basics 198
Mustard Seed Sauce

1kg rabbit carcass, chopped small
30g carrot, peeled and chopped small
30g celery, peeled and chopped small
30g onion, peeled and chopped small
750ml white wine
1 bunch tarragon
1.5 litres white chicken stock (basics 1)
500ml brown chicken stock (basics 2)
650ml whipping cream
salt and pepper, to taste

TO FINISH
20g tarragon, finely diced
20g chervil, chopped
10g white mustard seed, soaked
10g red mustard seed, soaked
frothed milk

METHOD

Lightly caramelise the rabbit carcass in a heavy-based frying pan, then drain through a colander. In the same frying pan, gently fry the carrots, celery and onions until they take a little colour, then drain through the colander. Deglaze the pan with 100ml of the white wine and transfer this and 800g of bones to a large pan. Cover with the remaining ingredients except the reserved bones, one-third of the bunch of tarragon and the cream. Bring the sauce to the boil and simmer gently for 2–3 hours, skimming as you go.

Pass the sauce through a colander and return to the empty pan. Add the reserved bones and tarragon, bring back to the boil and simmer for a further 2 hours, continuing to skim. Pass through a fine sieve and then a through a muslin cloth.

Return to a clean pan and reduce by three-quarters, to a heavy sauce consistency. Add the whipping cream and bring to a gentle simmer. Season to taste.

To finish, heat the sauce, add the herbs and seeds and then fold in the frothed milk.

Basics 199
Red Rabbit Sauce

1kg rabbit carcass, chopped small
30g onion, peeled and chopped small
30g carrot, peeled and chopped small
30g celery, peeled and chopped small
40g butter
50 shallots
100g button mushrooms, washed and sliced
25g cream
1.5 litres brown chicken stock (basics 2)
500ml veal stock (basics 3)
750ml red wine, reduced by two-thirds
1 bunch tarragon

METHOD

In a heavy-based frying pan, heavily caramelise the rabbit carcass with a little oil, then drain through a colander. In another frying pan, caramelise the onion, carrot and celery. When they have a good colour, finish with 20g of the butter, then drain through a colander. Lastly, make a fondue with the shallots and mushrooms by cooking them in a heavy-based pan over a medium heat until nicely caramelised. Finish with the remaining butter and drain through a colander.

Add all the ingredients to a large saucepan, reserving 200g of the rabbit carcass and one-third of the bunch of tarragon. Bring the ingredients to the boil and simmer for 2–3 hours, skimming as you go. Pass the sauce through a colander and return to the empty pan, then add the reserved bones and tarragon. Bring the sauce back to the boil and simmer for another 2–3 hours, while continuing to skim.

Pass the sauce through a fine sieve and then through muslin, and return to a clean pan. Reduce to a sauce consistency.

Basics 200
Herb Butter

125g butter, softened
40g tarragon, picked

METHOD

Place the butter and tarragon in a Thermomix and blitz until the tarragon has disintegrated and turned the butter green.

Basics 201
Moroccan Lamb Marinade

5g coriander seed, roasted
4g cumin seed, roasted
1 large pinch saffron
5g black peppercorns
4g juniper berries
25g orange zest
15g lemon zest
8g rosemary
50g garlic
15g coriander stalk
150g olive oil

METHOD

This recipe makes enough to marinate 20 lamb rumps but is not easily made in smaller batches, so portion it into bags and freeze for later.

Put all the ingredients in a Thermomix and blitz to a smooth paste, scraping the sides of the bowl as you go. To marinate the lamb rumps, rub in the paste and allow to marinate in the refrigerator for 24 hours.

Basics 202
Mushroom Duxelles

1 shallot, peeled and finely sliced
1 clove garlic, crushed
25g butter
600g flat mushrooms

METHOD

Sweat the shallot and garlic in the butter until soft. Meanwhile, peel the mushrooms and break into quarters, discarding the stalks. Add the mushrooms to the pan and cook over a medium heat until the mushrooms have released all their liquid and the mixture is dry. Put in a food processor and blitz to a very coarse paste. Season to taste.

Basics 203
Saffron Dressing

1 clove garlic
1 large pinch saffron
75g hot water
225g olive oil
100g white wine vinegar
salt and pepper, to taste

METHOD

Infuse the garlic clove and the saffron in the water for 15–20 minutes. Add the remaining ingredients and season to taste.

Finish by straining.

Basics 204
Red Wine Shallots

500g banana shallots, peeled and
finely sliced
250g red wine
150g sugar

METHOD

Put all the ingredients in a pan
and reduce until all the liquid has
evaporated. Season to taste.

Basics 205
Duck Stock

750g duck bones, all excess fat removed
100ml olive oil
1 onion, roughly chopped
1 celery stick
1 cinamon stick
1 star anise
50g fresh ginger, roughly chopped
1 bay leaf
750ml red wine
2 litres white chicken stock (basics 1)
1 litre brown chicken stock (basics 2)

METHOD

Sauté the duck bones in the olive
oil until golden brown. Add the
onion and celery and colour for
2–3 minutes, then pour off any
excess fat. Add the cinnamon,
anise, ginger, bay and red wine
and reduce by half. Add the stocks,
bring to the boil and skim. Simmer
for 45 minutes, then pass through a
fine sieve.

Basics 206
Duck Cherry Sauce

500g mallard bones, finely chopped and
all excess fat removed
100ml olive oil
1 large onion, roughly chopped
1 carrot, roughly chopped
2 juniper berries
2 star anise
6 black peppercorns, crushed
500ml red wine
500ml ruby port
1 litre duck stock (basics 205)
500ml white chicken stock (basics 1)
1kg stoned black cherries, roughly
chopped
50ml kirsch
salt and pepper, to taste

METHOD

Saute the mallard bones in the olive
oil until golden brown. Add the
onion and carrot and cook out for a
further 5 minutes. Pour off any excess
fat, and remove 10% of the bones to
refresh the sauce at a later stage. Add
the juniper, anise and peppercorns,
the red wine and port, and reduce by
half. Add the stocks, bring to the boil,
skim and reduce by half. Remove
from the heat and add 900g of the
cherries. Allow to infuse for 2 hours,
then strain through a fine sieve.

To finish, add the reserved bones,
cherries and kirsch, bring back to
the boil and simmer for 10 minutes.
Correct seasoning and strain through
a fine sieve.

Basics 207
Braised Chicory

4 large Belgian endives
1 litre white chicken stock (basics 1)
2 sprigs thyme
25g sugar
salt and pepper, to taste

METHOD

Gently simmer the endive in the
chicken stock, thyme and sugar for
8–10 minutes, until tender, and
season to taste. Allow to cool in the
liquor.

Basics 208
Red Mullet Farce

250g red mullet meat
100g chorizo
30g stoned black olives
20g fresh red mullet livers
30g dry breadcrumbs
a few sprigs of chopped fresh coriander
1 egg

METHOD

Finely mince all the ingredients
together. Mix well

Basics 209
Chanterelle à la Crème

50g chopped shallot
25g finely chopped garlic
250g unsalted butter
75g plain flour
200ml milk
200ml whipping cream
500g chanterelle mushrooms,
cleaned thoroughly
salt and pepper, to taste

METHOD

Sauté the shallot and garlic in
150g of the butter for 4–5 minutes
without colouring. Add the flour
and stir until smooth. Cook over a
low heat for 5 minutes. Gradually
add the milk and cream and stir
until smooth. Cook over a medium
heat until reduced by half.

Sauté the mushrooms in the
remaining butter. Cook out until all
the liquid has evaporated, then add
to the cream mixture and correct
seasoning.

Basics 210
Truffle Dressing

100ml truffle bouillon
350g fresh mayonnaise (basics 61)
75g Perigord truffle, finely chopped
1 tsp white truffle oil
salt and pepper, to taste

METHOD

Gently warm the truffle bouillon, then whisk all the ingredients together until emulsified. Adjust the consistency with a touch of water if required. Season to taste.

Basics 211
Pain d'Epice

560g milk
1kg honey
1 lemon, zested
1 orange, zested
40g baking powder
480g plain flour
480g rye flour
30g ginger
30g cinnamon
15g nutmeg, freshly grated
30g star anise
200g caster sugar
12 eggs

METHOD

Gently warm the milk, honey and zests just enough to melt the honey.

Sieve all the dry ingredients except the sugar into a large bowl.

Whisk the sugar and eggs in a food mixer until they reach a light and fluffy sabayon; this will take about 20 minutes.

Mix the milk and flour together to form a smooth paste, then fold in the sabayon. Don't be too gentle with the sabayon, as the end product doesn't want to be too light.

Split the mixture between 6 lined square tins about 20cm × 20cm and bake at 120°C for 4 hours until a deep golden brown. The

longer you leave them in the oven at this stage, the easier they will be to slice.

Remove from the tins and allow to go almost cold, then peel off the baking parchment.

Basics 212
Gingerbread

1kg honey
560g milk
1 lemon, zested
1 orange, zested
40g baking powder
480g plain flour
480g rye flour
60g ginger
15g nutmeg, freshly grated
30g star anise
200g caster sugar
12 eggs

METHOD

Gently warm the milk, honey and zests just enough to melt the honey.

Sieve all the dry ingredients except the sugar into a large bowl.

Whisk the sugar and eggs in a food mixer until they reach a light and fluffy sabayon; this will take about 20 minutes.

Mix the milk and flour together to form a smooth paste, then fold in the sabayon. Don't be too gentle with the sabayon, as the end product doesn't want to be too light.

Split the mixture between 6 lined square tins about 20cm × 20cm and bake at 120°C for 4 hours until a deep golden brown. The longer you leave them in the oven at this stage, the easier they will be to slice.

Remove from the tins and allow to go almost cold, then peel off the baking parchment.

Basics 213
Gruyère Gratin

100g grated Gruyère cheese
75g Parmesan cheese
250ml double cream
1 tbsp Dijon mustard
1 sprig rosemary
salt and pepper, to taste

METHOD

Place all the ingredients in a saucepan and heat until the cheese has melted. Use as required

Basics 214
Lemon Sorbet

4 lemons, juiced and zested
375g water
250g caster sugar

METHOD

Place the juice, zest, water and sugar in a saucepan. Cook to hard ball stage. Strain through a chinois and cool. Pour into a Pacojet container and freeze at −21°C.

Finish on the Pacojet machine and store in the freezer

Basics 215
Elderflower & Raspberry Jelly

500g sugar syrup (basics 180)
10 leaves gelatine, soaked
300g champagne
125g white wine
100g elderflower cordial
24 fresh raspberries

METHOD

Warm the syrup, and dissolve the gelatine. Add the champagne, white wine and cordial. Mix well and strain through a chinois. Flood the base of a container 20cm × 20cm with jelly, ½ cm deep. Set in the refrigerator on a level surface.

When set, place raspberries on the jelly 3cm apart; before placing them on the set jelly, dip the bases in the liquid jel to make them stay in place. Set in the refrigerator.

Pour over the excess jelly to cover the raspberries, and set in the refrigerator.

Using a cutter approx 2.5 cm diameter, cut around the raspberries leaving them encased in jelly

Remove and place on a small tray and reserve in the refrigerator.

Baics 216
Apricot Espuma

600g apricot purée
3 leaves gelatine, soaked
350g white peach purée (basics 165)
50g peach schnapps

METHOD

Heat 100g of the apricot purée. Add the gelatine and dissolve until smooth.

Mix with the rest of the apricot purée, and incorporate the peach purée and the alcohol. Pass through a chinois.

Place in a Chantilly whipper, add 2 shots of gas and shake well.

Leave in the refrigerator until required.

Basics 217
Candied Pistachio Nuts

70g egg whites
70g caster sugar
70g green pistachio nuts

METHOD

Whisk the egg whites gently together with the sugar. Fold in the pistachio nuts. Bake in a shallow stainless steel tray at 150°C, turning occasionally.

Remove from the oven when lightly golden brown.

Basics 218
Blackcurrant Jelly

60g water
35g sugar syrup (basics 180)
1 leaf gelatine, soaked
40g blackcurrant purée

METHOD

Boil together the water and the sugar syrup. Remove from the heat and dissolve the gelatine. Whisk in the purée. Pass through a chinois, then pour into a container 7cm × 14cm and leave to set in the refrigerator.

Gently warm the base, and unmould onto a chopping board. Using a warm knife, cut into 12 rectangles 2cm × 3cm.

Reserve in the refrigerator until required

Basics 219
Blackcurrant Sauce

200g blackcurrant purée
30g caster sugar
10g lemon juice

METHOD

Bring the blackcurrant purée and the sugar to the boil. Remove from the heat and add the lemon juice.

Pass through a chinois, and reserve until cold.

Basics 220
Coconut Tuile

ingredients as for plain tuile (basics 126)
15g desiccated coconut

METHOD

Add the desiccated coconut to the mixture and proceed as for plain tuile.

Basics 221
Chocolate Tuile

100g orange juice
200g icing sugar
40g T55 flour
20g cocoa powder
120g melted butter

METHOD

Mix the orange juice and the sugar together. Sieve the flour and cocoa powder and add to the orange juice and sugar mixture. Add the cold melted butter.

Spread onto a silpat mat. Cook in the oven at 170°C for 7–8 minutes.

Basics 222
Blood Orange Pâte de Fruit

800g blood orange purée
935g caster sugar
15g pectin
185g glucose syrup
15g lemon juice
cola sherbet

METHOD

Place the purée into a suitable size saucepan and bring to the boil. Mix 85g of the sugar with the pectin powder and whisk quickly into the purée. Remove from the heat.

Place the remaining sugar and the glucose in a saucepan and saturate with water. Cook to 155°C.

Add the purée to the cooked sugar and mix well; cook to 107°C. Add the lemon juice, mix well and pour onto a lined tray 8cm × 4cm.

Leave to set. Cut into 1cm cubes, and roll in cola sherbet.

Basics 223
Orange Reduction

300g orange juice
75g caster sugar

METHOD

Place the juice and the sugar in a pan and bring to the boil. Reduce the liquor by half.

Pass through a chinois, and reserve until cold.

Basics 224
White Coffee Ice Cream

240g whole coffee beans
300g whipping cream
1kg milk
160g egg yolks
240g caster sugar

METHOD

Roast the coffee beans in the oven. Add to the cream and milk and allow to infuse for 24 hours.

Strain off the coffee beans, and place the infused milk and cream in a saucepan. Emulsify the yolks with the sugar, and cook as for an anglaise (see basics 177). Pass through a chinois, and cool over ice.

Fill up Pacojet containers to under maximum level and freeze to −21°C. Place on the Pacojet machine to finish the ice cream.

Basics 225
Grue de Cacao Tuile

300g caster sugar
100g glucose
250g unsalted butter
100g milk
5g pectin n.h.
50g caster sugar
300g grue nib

METHOD

Place 250g of the sugar in a pan with the glucose, butter and milk and bring to the boil. Whisk in the pectin and the remaining sugar until smooth, then reboil. Cook to 103°C. Mix in the grue nib.

Place on silicone paper and roll to the thickness of the grue nib. Bake in the oven at 170°C for 12 minutes, turning the trays once.

When baked, rest for 2–3 minutes, then cut to size. Store in cool dry conditions until needed.

Basics 226
Lamb stock

1kg lamb bones, roughly chopped
100ml olive oil
100g chopped onion
50g chopped garlic
300g fresh plum tomatoes
2 sprigs rosemary
1 sprig thyme
500ml white wine
2 litres white chicken stock (basics 1)

METHOD

Caramelise the lamb bones in the olive oil until golden brown. Add the onion and garlic and cook out for a further 5 minutes. Strain off any excess fat, add the tomatoes and herbs and cook over a medium heat for 10 minutes.

Add the white wine and reduce by half. Add the stock and bring to the boil. Skim and simmer for 45 minutes, then pass through a fine sieve.

Basics 227
Fennel Purée

3 heads fennel
75g butter
5g fennel seed
500ml milk
500ml cream
salt and pepper, to taste

METHOD

Finely chop the fennel. Melt 25g of the butter in a large saucepan and add the fennel and fennel seed. Cover with a lid and cook on a low heat until the fennel is very soft. Stir occasionally to prevent the bottom from catching.

Cover with the milk and cream and simmer for 20 minutes. Drain the fennel well and transfer to a Thermomix; blitz until smooth. With the machine still running, add the remaining butter and allow to emulsify. Season to taste.

Basics 228
Cooked Foie Gras

1 loaf foie gras
15ml white port
15ml cognac
15ml Madeira
pink salt
salt
sugar

METHOD

Allow the foie gras to come to room temperature. Split the loaf into two lobes, then with the handle of a spoon gently butterfly the foie gras, removing the veins as you go. It is important to remove all the veins as they will make the end product bitter.

Season the foie gras with all the remaining ingredients and allow to marinate for 2 hours; turn and season the other side and allow to marinate for a further hour. Transfer to a sealable bag and poach at 45°C for 8 minutes until very soft.

Allow to cool in the refrigerator until pliable. Transfer to a tin lined with cling film and press in the refrigerator until set.

Basics 229
Crispy Rissotto

40g finely chopped shallot
25g butter
250g risotto rice
640ml water
1 sprig rosemary
210g Parmesan cheese
salt and pepper, to taste
pané, to finish

METHOD

Sauté the shallots in the butter for 2–3 minutes without colouring. Stir in the rice and mix well. Add the water and rosemary, and cook gently until the rice is al dente. Remove from the heat, and allow to sit for 5 minutes then stir in the Parmesan. Make sure that the cheese is mixed in well and check the seasoning.

Pour the risotto into a lined baking tray – the risotto rice should be spread evenly and be 3–4cm thick. Cover and allow to cool in the refrigerator for 2–3 hours.

When cold, cut into even-sized cubes and pané (flour, egg, breadcrumb). Deep fry at 180°C for 2–3 minutes until golden brown.

Basics 230
Liquorice Sauce

500g chicken bones, finely chopped and all excess fat removed
100ml olive oil
1 large onion, roughly chopped
1 carrot, roughly chopped
2 juniper berries
2 star anise
4 liquorice sticks, crushed
6 black peppercorns, crushed
1 litre red wine
250ml ruby port
1 litre brown chicken stock (basics 2)
500ml white chicken stock (basics 1)

METHOD

Saute the chicken bones in the olive oil until golden brown. Add the onion and carrot and cook out for a further 5 minutes, then pour off any excess fat. Remove 10% of the bones to refresh the sauce at a later stage. Add the liquorice, juniper, anise and peppercorns, the red wine and port, and reduce by half. Add the stocks, bring to the boil, skim and reduce by half. Remove from the heat and strain through a fine sieve.

To finish, add the reserved bones, bring back to the boil and simmer for 10 minutes. Correct seasoning and strain through a fine sieve. Reduce to the desired consistency.

Basics 231
Caviar Dressing

8 medium native oysters
25ml Cabernet Sauvignon vinegar or red wine vinegar
50ml groundnut oil
25g salmon roe
25g oscietra caviar
salt and pepper, to taste

METHOD

Dry the oysters on kitchen paper to remove excess water. Place the oysters, vinegar and oil in food processor and blend until smooth. Pass through a fine sieve. Lastly add the salmon roe and caviar. Season to taste.

Make the dressing the day you want to use it.

Basics 232
Charlotte Artichoke Mousse

500g Jerusalem artichokes, peeled
500ml whipping cream
5 leaves gelatine, soaked
7 egg whites
salt and pepper, to taste

METHOD

Grate the artichokes into a pan and cover with the cream. Bring to the boil and cook quickly until soft.

While the cream is still hot, mix in the gelatine and then transfer to a Thermomix and blitz until smooth. Transfer the liquid to a metal bowl over ice and allow to set, stirring occasionally.

In a separate bowl, whisk the egg whites until firm then fold through the artichoke mixture. Season to taste.

2 litres water
2 lemons, juiced
5g ascorbic acid
8 poivrade artichokes
30ml olive oil
2 banana shallots
4 cloves garlic
10 black peppercorns
thyme
bay leaf
125ml white wine
50ml white wine vinegar

METHOD

Mix the water, lemon juice and ascorbic acid together.

To prepare the artichokes, start by snapping off the hard outer leaves, breaking them as close to the head as possible. Continue this process until all that is left is the delicate inner leaves at the top of the head.

The next stage is to peel away the remaining dark green skin. Start halfway up the stalk and peel up towards head, then flip the artichoke over and peel the other half of the stalk, until only cream flesh is remaining. Finally trim the remaining leaves just above the choke.

Put the prepared artichokes into the acidulated water while you are preparing the others.

In a medium-sized pan, fry the shallots, garlic, peppercorns and herbs until soft but not coloured. Add the wine and vinegar and reduce by half. Add the artichokes and cover with the acidulated water, then bring to the boil and simmer for 3 minutes, until tender. Season to taste and allow to cool in the liquor.

'Alan Murchison's outstanding cooking
at his quite exceptional restaurant,
his thorough experience of teaching
to cook and his down-to-earth
common sense rare in top-rate chefs
are an exceptional combination coming
to life in this valuable book.'

Egon Ronay, Food Critic

'Chef Alan, sometimes genius,
mostly maniac.'

Ania Gniazdowska, Restaurant Manager, L'Ortolan

food for thought food for thought food for thought
food for thought food for thought food for thought
food for thought food for thought food for thought
food for thought food for thought food for thought
food for thought food for thought food for thought
food for thought food for thought food for thought
food for thought food for thought food for thought
food for thought food for thought food for thought
food for thought food for thought food for thought
food for thought food for thought food for thought
food for thought food for thought food for thought
food for thought food for thought food for thought
food for thought food for thought food for thought
food for thought food for thought food for thought

alan murchison alan murchison alan murchiso

food for thought food for thought food for though
food for thought food for thought food for though
food for thought food for thought food for though
food for thought food for thought food for though
food for thought food for thought food for though
food for thought food for thought food for though
food for thought food for thought food for though
food for thought food for thought food for though
food for thought food for thought food for though
food for thought food for thought food for though
food for thought food for thought food for though
food for thought food for thought food for though
food for thought food for thought food for though
food for thought food for thought food for though
food for thought food for thought food for though